Mental Health In The Music Industry

Written by
Austin Mardon & Reinette Schabert

Edited by
Catherine Mardon & Jessica Jutras

GM★
P R E S S

First Printing: 2021

Typeset and Cover Design by Kim Huynh

ISBN: 978-1-77369-672-0
EBook ISBN: 978-1-77369-673-7

Golden Meteorite Press
103 11919 82 St NW
Edmonton, AB T5B 2W3
www.goldenmeteoritepress.com

GM★
P R E S S

Table of Contents

Introduction

Mental health has become a topic of concern in the music industry. Though mental health is an aspect of all people, and not just musicians, life in the music industry can exacerbate things.

> "Money is tight while they work long and weird hours, travel incessantly, are isolated from their friends and family at home, and have ample access to drinks and drugs. They write, record, release, and promote, and then repeat the cycle over and over again. And now, more than ever, the industry demands constant content, lest they be forgotten in the ocean of songs hitting Spotify every Friday. But then they get in the van and, especially in Canada, drive absurd distances between low-paying gigs for a tour they likely had to book themselves" (Raine 2019).

In this book, we will explore many topics that tie into mental health in the music industry. These topics will include: general and common mental illnesses in musicians, alcoholism, drug addictions, suicide rates, imposter syndrome, music performance anxiety, social influences, female representation in the music industry, how music impacts our brains, and where to find help and supports.

"Music is a ubiquitous, social phenomenon that has been found in cultures as far back in history as can be traced" (Phelps 2014, 28). It has and always will be a part of our society. It plays a role in our identities, it has a major impact on listeners, and it affects the next generation of musicians and music listeners. For the amount of impact that music has on our lives, it is concerning how little we take care of the people who are providing this service. It is also concerning how separated performers and listeners have become when musicality is a universal skill that all humans are born with.

1

The final goal of this book is to encourage more mental health advocates through awareness and understanding, as well as to point to community involvement in music as a way to support the music community as a whole.

Each chapter will also take a look at the impact on youth and young musicians. Much of the information being explored in this book is based around the idea of bringing awareness and understanding to issues in order to pave a better way forwards for people growing up today. "Creativity is particularly important for young people and students today, both for solving the problems society faces and assuaging their existential fears… young people need to know that they're living at a time when their creativity really matters." (Henriksen and Mishra 2020, 6). Mental health support can and should start being accessible for people at young ages. Especially in the education system, "most children are locked into age-groupings for learning, rather than being supported based on individual passions, interests, abilities or needs" (6). Creative development needs stronger connections to individual temperaments and real world experiences. Recognizing the need for musical training is one way to give students more access to creative experiences. "Musical training doesn't just teach you music, it teaches you history, in playing pieces from other eras. It teaches you about world religions [and] about culture" (4). The music industry could and should be so much more than just the musicians who make a living in it. Every human is born with musicality. And every human can and should be able to participate in music making.

Chapter 1.
Mental Illnesses in Musicians

Introducing the Topic

Mental illness permeates every facet of human existence, and each sub-community has unique problems. Mental illnesses, left untreated, can culminate to become larger problems, and eventually can lead to harming self or harming others (High Focus Centers 2018). Musicians in North America who have mental illnesses often struggle to obtain proper help due to barriers of both stigma and lifestyle. Increasing awareness around mental illness and understanding its impact (both on oneself and on others), can help reduce stigma and feelings of shame, and increase the efficacy of implemented supports.

Studying mental illness within a general group of people can be difficult due to the potential spectrum of type and severity. Many resources are reported on an individual basis rather than through academic double-blind randomized control studies (Kaufman and Sternberg 2010, 382). Therefore there will be some juxtapositions between academic writings and findings, and reports done on communities of musicians.

There are many types and categories of mental illnesses, and there are many roles included in the music industry. Focus will be placed on the mental illnesses that are most often currently associated within the music industry. The majority of case studies mentioned will be women in the music industry who have been outspoken about their own mental health. "Both levels of self-reported anxiety and depression were higher among our female than our male respondents" (Gross and Musgrave 2020, 35). Due to the underrepresentation of females in various media, they will be given precedent in this paper.

Depression is one of the major concerns coming out within the music community, as well as the difficulty of obtaining consistent support and help. Contributing factors are "financial challenges… anti-social working hours, touring schedules and an 'always on' mentality driven by [an] oversupply of music and lack of boundaries" (Gross and Musgrave 2020). Though resources and aid are not yet a regularity in a musician's career, there are resources becoming increasingly available and more readily accessible specifically to the musician. It is important to understand what mental illness is, how it affects musicians, and what trends both academic studies and interviews have shown in order to continue to create an inclusive community that fosters an environment that is supportive of mental health.

A Common Misperception

The myth that mental illness and musicians go hand in hand must first be discounted. Mental illness refers to clinical disorders such as personality disorders, thought disorders and mood disorders; musicians referring to all people involved in professional music making. The fallacy that has been created through public opinion and published material on sensationalized figures is that if one is in a creative field, like music, then one is likely to have a mental illness (Kaufman and Sternberg 2010, 385). Whereas the opposite holds more truth, if one has a mental illness, they are likely to be creative. However, the general concept of creativity in itself creates a problem in properly studying this potential connection: "research that samples creative people and assesses mental illness affords very different conclusions than research that samples the mentally ill and assesses creativity" (390).

As pointed out in one study, it is difficult to have an accurate representation of mental illness in musicians due to the "diagnoses [being] made posthumously and using loose and inconsistent diagnostic criteria" (Pavitra et al 2007, 34). In addition, "it is possible that the creative persons with dramatic lives and early deaths are more likely to become eminent and have biographies written about them" (35). There is not enough data to make a claim comparing the people who make a living in the industry with people who do not make a living in a creative field. "The world has at least one too many movies about tortured painters, narcissistic architects, depressed poets, and drug-addicted musicians" (Kaufman and Sternberg 2010, 381). Kaufman goes on to discuss the futility of case studies among the creative population due to over-generalization (382). Nor is there enough data to truly study if mental illness is a factor of being a musician, or a precursor to being a musician.

"Creativity and mental illness merely co-occur. Third variables - such as childhood experiences, socioeconomic status, peer groups, and normal personality traits - cause both creativity and mental illness" (Kaufman 385). In specifically identifying mental illness in musicians, while decreasing stigma through understanding and increased support, there is a chance to reduce detrimental outcomes.

However, there are studies that show musicians, among the people who work in a creative field, have better potential coping skills (Pavitra et al 2007, 37). When working towards an end goal of a community fostering mental health, it is not the idea that musicians may have a higher rate of mental illness that is important... It is the idea that people who have mental illness may find coping skills and strategies through the creative process. This idea can flip the stigma associated with a person who has a mental illness: instead of being ashamed that they struggle with a mental illness in their creative field, they can find ownership in the fact that their creative field has become a medium to minimize the negative effects of mental illness and can be a precursor to help others who struggle with a similar mental illness find coping skills and strategies. "If there would've been less tip-toeing and avoidance, and people were straight-up understanding of mental illness and substance abuse... things may have been different" (Frehsee 2020).

Case Studies

Using public figure acknowledgements of mental illness in conjunction with academic studies is a way to start to close the gap in understanding the implications of why knowledge and de-stigmatization of mental illness is important. The resounding messages shared over and over again can build community by acknowledging fears around changed public image, the negative impacts of mental illness on personal lives, and using a desire to help others as a motivating factor.

Alanis Morissette, talking about her postpartum depression, talks about the difficulties normally hidden from public eyes: "sleep deprivation. Fogginess. Physical pain. Isolation. Anxiety. Cortisol. Recovery from childbirth... Marriage. All kinds of PTSD triggers... [postpartum depression] is still a sneaky monkey with a machete" (Chan 2021).

Ariana Grande speaks about her own struggles with PTSD and anxiety following the bombing during one of her 2017 shows: "I've always had anxiety. I've never really spoken about it because I thought everyone had it, but when I got home from the tour it was the most severe I think it's ever been… Here's to ending the stigma around mental health and normalizing asking for help" (Chan 2021).

Bebe Rexha talks about her bipolar disorder diagnosis: "for the longest time I didn't understand why I felt so sick. Why I felt lows that made me not want to leave my house or be around people and why I felt highs that wouldn't let me sleep, wouldn't let me stop working or creating music. Now I know why… Honesty is a form of self love" (Chan 2021).

Beyoncé talks about how she took a year off to deal with her mental health: "it was beginning to get fuzzy – I couldn't even tell which day or which city I was at… Women have to take the time to focus on our mental health – take time for self, for the spiritual, without feeling guilty or selfish" (Kheraj 2018).

Demi Lovato has been candid about their battles with eating disorders, self-harm and bipolar disorder: "I just think mental illness is something people need to learn more about and the stigma needs to be taken away from… This is an ongoing process and the hardest part about these diseases is that they're things that I'm going to have to face every day for the rest of my life… I stand here today as proof that you can live a normal and empowered life with mental illness" (Kheraj 2018).

Elle King shares her struggle with PTSD and depression: "I think that reaching out saved my life. I don't wanna think of any other outcome that could have happened. I feel like the more I talk about it, maybe it could reach somebody… reach somebody that feels alone" (Chan 2021).

Janet Jackson says, "I struggled with depression. The struggle was intense… Low self-esteem might be rooted in childhood feelings of inferiority. It could relate to failing to meet impossibly high standards. And of course there are always the societal issues of racism and sexism… Put it all together and depression is a tenacious and scary condition" (Chan 2021).

Kristen Bell, when speaking about her depression, talks about how "it's important for [her] to be candid about this so people in a similar situation can realize that they are not worthless and that they do have something to offer. We all do" (Chan 2021).

Mariah Carey shares her fears around her bipolar II diagnosis: "until recently I lived in denial and isolation and in constant fear someone would expose me. It was too heavy a burden to carry and I simply couldn't do that anymore" (Chan 2021).

Naomi Judd opens up about her severe depression diagnosis: "they see me in rhinestones, you know, with glitter in my hair, like that really is who I am... But then I would come home and not leave the house for three weeks, and not get out of my pyjamas, and not practice normal hygiene. It was really bad" (Chan 2021).

In hearing more and more from public figures opening up about their mental illnesses, one can only wonder how many more musicians struggle with their own mental illness but without the public platform. "Record Union shared the results of a survey conducted with almost 1,500 musicians. The report found that more than 73% of independent music makers suffer from symptoms of mental illness, and that anxiety and depression were the most commonly experienced negative emotions in relation to music creation" (Barnby 2019). These kinds of statistics call for more attention to be brought to the underlying issues. And if the situation makes it difficult to study root causes, or if there is not a root cause and merely being human puts one at risk... then education and de-stigmatization are even more important in creating a community that fosters mental health.

Help within the Musician's Lifestyle

In the meantime, there are some resources available to musicians. These resources are often only accessed if the person seeking help is educated. "Our collective understanding of the deep connections between physical and mental health, and music, has improved considerably, support is the crucial difference" (Wassenberg 2019). More information on what other support is available will be explored in Chapter 10. It is important to note that the public opinion, which comes from their own awareness and understanding, still has a big impact on musicians getting help... or feeling like they should get help.

"The myth of the tortured genius still — unfortunately — looms large in the public imagination. Some would point out the splendid output of all those brilliant composers who worked while suffering their various mental health issues. More pertinent, however, would be to wonder how many more masterpieces they would have bestowed on musical history if their illnesses had been understood, and treated rather than ignored" (Wassenberg 2019).

One Canadian mental wellness fund, the Unison Benevolent Fund, provides "counselling services and emergency financial relief to Canadian musicians and industry professionals in times of need" (Raine 2019). It was set up by Canadian indie label owner, Versteeg, as a response to his own experiences in the field (2019). There are "initiatives like Bell Let's Talk Day or the Canadian Mental Health Association's Mental Health Week, politicians, artists, athletes, and common Canadians are talking more openly and publicly about their own experiences" (2019), which are contributing to the shift in public acceptance of mental illness, however there is still a gap to cover.

With the ubiquity of music in the North American community, the financial burden musicians often face is shocking. Raine writes about how the corporations profiting from the music industry should have a larger role in protecting the musicians (2019). "It's kind of the responsibility of everyone in the industry to level the playing field a bit for the artists who are really the basis of everything the music industry is able to do" (2019).

Williams offers some resource advice for musicians concerning caring for their mental health: build a relationship with a local therapist, check if your local university has a counselling centre open to the public, work with your family doctor, attend peer-led groups such as NA or AA, and delve into written material like self-help books, often found at local libraries (2019). Williams also offers some lifestyle changes for musicians, all of which can be utilized within a variety of musician typical lifestyles: mindfulness activities like meditation, increasing physical activity and healthy eating, taking alcohol off your hospitality rider, finding a therapist who is available to do phone session, and nurture friendships and interpersonal relationships (2019).

Barnby outlines some factors that affect the mental health of musicians, "there are three pretty consistent reasons independent musicians face mental health challenges… financial instability… pressure to perform and resonate with audiences… [and] a culture of self-medication and drug abuse in the music industry" (2019). Barnby offers a solution for touring musicians and their team in the form of "a team member that's dedicated to psychological support" (2019). Barnby also leans into the idea of fostering mental health through creating a community of people through online platforms and "online resources where musicians can connect with and learn from each other about the things they encounter" (2019).

Impact on Youth and Young Musicians

Youth and young musicians will continuously be the test of what current changes are actually being made in the industry. They will be the ones to inherit any problems, as well as any solutions that are being made today. This is why it is important to have supports for mental health available from a young age. Within the music industry, to access and impact young musicians, this has to start with music teachers, universities, colleges, band camps, venues, and parents. It starts with education. It starts with awareness. It starts with the public figures and adults being willing to talk, and being willing to listen.

Concluding Thoughts

As humans, there will always be illnesses of all kinds present. Having a mental illness should not stop someone from pursuing a career, or from accessing help while continuing to work in their chosen field. As Kheraj mentions in his article, "people with mental health problems say that stigma and discrimination had a negative impact on their lives" (2018). This does not have to be the case with proper resources available. De-stigmatization can be achieved through increased awareness and understanding; and a willingness to listen. The advocacy of public figures willing to share their stories is a step in the right direction. In order to elicit involvement of corporations and government, more academic studies should be undertaken. A willingness to be a friend and an ally of people who have a mental illness is something every individual can do by increasing their knowledge of various mental illnesses. Increased community support for people with mental illness can remove barriers to mental health support by de-stigmatizing accessing mental health supports.

Chapter 2.
Alcoholism in Musicians

Introducing the Topic

Mental illness was discussed in the previous chapter. Another common aspect that musicians deal with is substance abuse. Alcoholism will be discussed in this chapter, followed by drug addiction in Chapter 3.

Careers in the music industry often involve a lifestyle factor of drinking. However, like the topic of mental illness, it is difficult to study the complicated topic of alcoholism in musicians. It cannot be reduced to isolated roots. Alcoholism is prevalent in North American culture in general (Ingraham 2017). The North American music industry being a part of that culture, therefore, also has ties to alcoholism. The correlation between alcoholism and musicians may not be a disputed fact, however there are studies that associate "creativity with various forms of psychopathology, including mood disorders, schizotypal thinking, [and] alcohol abuse" (Carson 2014). There are two main reasons for understanding the effect of alcoholism in the music industry: the impact on mental health, and the impact on youth and young musicians.

Correlation Between Alcoholism and Musicians

The first question that must be asked is whether alcoholism in the music industry is a result of career lifestyle, modelling of other successful musicians, or a creative predisposition to addiction. Although there are not enough academic studies to support one thesis over another, it is likely to be a combination. As with all factors that affect mental health, like mental illness, understanding what to do with this burden on mental health must first begin with understanding what it is.

Terminology is important in understanding the difference between the varying levels of alcohol consumption. "Alcohol dependence, sometimes known as 'alcoholism,' is the most serious form of drinking problem and describes a strong, often uncontrollable, desire to drink" (Drinkaware 2021), the biggest difference lies in the effect on mental health. Alcohol abuse is different from alcohol dependence, and though both affect health and wellbeing, "people with alcohol abuse problems usually manage to carry on their lives with some semblance of normality, once dependence kicks in, the alcohol takes over" (2021).

In terms of music pop culture, "being a musician has often come with a series of default lifestyle expectations, ones of indulgence and recklessness, larger-than-life living, and a diligent pursuit of altered forms of consciousness" (Heath 2019). And not only are there lifestyle factors at work, there are also factors associated with working in a creative field: "these studies appear to indicate that highly creative individuals are at greater risk for certain disorders [like alcohol abuse] than are members of the general public" (Carson 2014). It is interesting to note that the very act of creativity, or exploring new ideas, known as novelty salience, is also "associated with creative personality, creative drive, alcohol abuse and addiction, and with bipolar states of hypomania and mania" (2014). In the chapter on mental illness in musicians, the case studies line up with these results.

To say that drinking any alcohol is bad is not correct. There are many people who have good mental health, and drink alcohol. There is also debate and discrepancies between where the threshold lies between the amount of appropriate alcohol intake. The focus here though, is to understand the part that alcohol plays in a musicians life, and its impact on their mental health. What are some of the indicators of alcohol negatively impacting mental health? And what does that mean for musicians?

Impact of Alcoholism on Mental Health

Alcohol dependency, or alcoholism, can induce anxiety, depression, and suicidal feelings (Drinkaware 2021). "This is because regular, heavy drinking interferes with neurotransmitters in our brains that are needed for good mental health... as we drink more, the impact on our brain function increases" (2021). The Drinkaware site also cites the correlation between alcohol dependency and psychiatric disorders, "particularly depression, anxiety, post-traumatic stress disorder, psychosis and drug misuse...

alcohol makes these disorders worse because it interferes with the chemical balance in our brains" (2021).

As musicians are humans, the effects of alcoholism on their mental health is the same as stated above. The case studies that follow are focused on representing females in the music industry. There are some general musicians cited with a quick overview of their relationship with alcohol, followed by some more in depth interviews with two musicians.

Case Studies

Amy Winehouse, an English singer-songwriter, "died from alcohol poisoning" (Hanson 2021).

Billie Holiday, a jazz singer, "was alcoholic most of her life [and] died of heart disease caused by cirrhosis of the liver from alcoholism" (Hanson 2021).

"Lana Del Rey, a singer-songwriter and producer, no longer drinks [and] works with an outreach program for people with alcohol and drug addictions" (Hanson 2021).

Soko, a French singer-songwriter who has been sober for 14 years, speaks on her life before sobriety:

> "I started going out to bars with my stepbrother when I was 13… then when I was 16, I started going out three, four times a week and then every night… once I woke up in some throw-up that was all red—I thought, 'I woke up in blood!' and was terrified. Then I realized I threw up wine… I was definitely having fun, and I felt like I was living life. I felt like that's what life was about" (Heath 2019).

Soko then speaks about why she decided to make a change:

> "I was hanging out with people a lot older than me, and I was looking at their lives, and so at 19 I was like, 'I don't want to be like you when I'm 30. I don't want to be like any of you. I'm super-ambitious, I want to be working, and I want to do something meaningful with my life'" (2019).

She then talks about the impact of sobriety on her life:

"I started making music. I started booking more films. Work became easy. I never had a hangover again, which was awesome... I can totally party. If I decide to go out, I can be out till 6 a.m. and be sober and be completely fine. But it needs to be the right time and the right place and the right people" (2019).

Soko has no fear of relapse, she values her health and her relationships over the lifestyle that once came with a drinking lifestyle (2019). She loves that "self-care is now finally a cool thing... when before, it was like you're a freak" (2019).

Julien Baker, a singer-songwriter six years sober, speaks on her life before sobriety and makes an important point on the societal differences between alcohol dependence in youth versus adults:

"I started smoking cigarettes when I was 12 years old... I would drink with [the older kids] and smoke weed with them. We would experiment with prescription drugs, and it got darker and darker until it wasn't necessarily a social thing anymore... I feel like many people struggled with the abuse of substances when they were adults, and I think that lends a gravity to them that is easily dismissed or obscured when you use substances as a child. That sort of falls into the paradigm of a debaucherous adolescent, sort of an irresponsible teenager. It's just portrayed as irresponsibility or recklessness, and it only starts to be labeled as a life-altering problem when you get into adulthood.... that cultural categorization of substance abuse as the taboo but expected misbehaviour of children contributed to me having a warped sort of denial about the substances I was using and approaching them cavalierly" (Heath 2019).

Baker makes a comment about her fears around her alcohol dependency and its impact on her mental health:

"I do have a little bit of trouble with candor around the things that I used to do. I think it's probably just resultant of shame and embarrassment and not wanting to be defined by the life that I used to live... The other fear is that when substances aren't there and I'm alone, I'm going to have confront something even scarier, which is myself and my own consciousness. Now I have to sit there and be with myself, and that is most terrifying of all... I was not having fun. I was very scared and uncomfortable and sad. But I didn't know how to name any

13

of those emotions. I was just doing it because that's what you do. Or that's what people around me were doing. It was more like a numbing agent, or an escape mechanism, I suppose" (Heath 2019).

Baker speaks about the importance of finding a community in her field that portrayed the lifestyle she wanted to pursue. She credits these relationships as a starting point to her finding help and support.

"It wasn't until I started going to DIY punk shows at a house that was substance-free, and the community of musicians there was largely substance-free. When I saw people that said, 'I just don't need that in my life,' it started a chain reaction in my mind. And they were all very kind to me for no reason—like, they would make me dinner, come pick me up when I got stranded, never asked any uncomfortable questions or made me feel judged or condescended to me. I think it started a natural catalyst in me of thinking that there's a better way to live" (2019).

Baker shares some of the difficulties she has in living sober:

"A difficulty of mine, and I think this is true for many addicts, is not transmuting your addiction to something else. When you have an addictive personality, you fixate upon things easily. Routines and behaviours, and ritual, become very important. When I quit substances, I started chain-smoking all the time. Then I quit smoking and I started running, but I would run constantly. Every time I wanted a cigarette...which was all the time. And I would sustain joint and tendon injuries" (Heath 2019).

Baker speaks on the benefits of sober life, the coping skills she's developed, and the importance of a having a healthy community:

"What I see in so many people that recover successfully, they become passionate about something. Like writing music, or painting, or hiking, or, like, building ships in bottles...and it either gives you a respite from the world or it gives you a creative outlet and it occupies your mind in a productive way... I think that faith and sobriety coincided for me because of how I saw the principles of faith performed; the people who were around in my life when I was at my very worst were not manipulating me with guilt, or throwing punitive scripture at me, they were showing me gentleness, patience, and mercy... In its most ideal form, faith values and acknowledges the manifold differences of individuals, but prizes the community in a way that decentralizes the focus from the self in a really healthy way that teaches empathy. Connection to a community is a deep human need, one that I think becomes even more important when in recovery. People find that in a lot of ways, in AA or support groups or music scenes or friend groups. To me, I think of all of these as what Christianity would call the body: people with different strengths and weaknesses that shoulder each other's burdens and give a little of themselves in service to one another so that they can reap the shared benefit and comfort" (2019).

These case studies and interviews are vital to understanding the role alcohol plays in the music industry. One common theme from the two longer interviews is the fear around making a change in a predetermined culture of drinking in the North American music scene. Another common theme is the desire to help others in a similar situation who want to positively impact their own mental health. An important note that Baker made in her interview was pointing out the discrepancies between teenage drinking seen as deviant rather than problematic, and the impact an earlier intervention could have made on her life.

Impact on Youth and Young Musicians

There are studies that show "people learn not only by direct experience but also by exposure to modelled behaviour, such as that represented in popular music" (Hilliard 2021). This is significant because of the role pop culture plays in North America. Especially in the music industry where "much of a musician's work takes place in bars and clubs" (Feibel 2020). Young musicians coming up in the industry are not only being inundated with the messaging in music, but also by the older musicians modelling drinking and partying. "Individuals that are exposed to representations of drinking and alcohol use are more likely to engage in those behaviours themselves if they are represented in a positive light and associated with desirable affluences" (Hilliard 2021). Alcohol in music and musicians drinking are "often associated with fun, power, money, respect, and sexual relationships which can all cause listeners to use alcohol in an effort to emulate their favourite musicians" (2021). In addition to this, "the music industry creates an environment where it not only glorifies drinking; it provides a structure for it" (Vincent 2014).

The impact on youth and young musicians can be detrimental. "Some have called on the industry itself to do more to support musicians who have quit drinking by taking steps such as providing more non-alcoholic options at concerts and events" (Feibel 2020). Having an understanding of what alcoholism is, when alcohol abuse turns to alcohol dependency, and how to get support, are all vital to building a community that fosters mental health.

Concluding Thoughts

Alcoholism may be a problem in all of North America, but it seems to prevail in the music industry due to the long standing lifestyle. "It's as if the constitution of an oak barrel is a key ingredient in the recipe for musical greatness" (Vincent 2014). Alcoholism is defined by a dependency on alcohol to the extent that it affects one's ability to function without it. Many artists have come forward speaking about the impact of alcoholism on their lives. These points have been reiterated: fear around judgement, desire for supportive community, and increased positive mental health in sobriety. "Young people are at particular risk of being negatively influenced by alcohol in music" (Hilliard 2021). Understanding and awareness of alcoholism helps set up youth and young musicians for success.

Chapter 3.
Drug Addictions in Musicians

Introducing the Topic

Addictions in general cover a wide range of substances and situations. Drug addiction is specifically what will be explored in this chapter. Drug addiction is "a chronic disease characterized by drug seeking and use that is compulsive, or difficult to control, despite harmful consequences" (NIDA 2018). As has been stated in previous chapters, there seems to be a correlation between addiction and musicians. The connections between mental illness, creativity, and addictions seem to have a relationship. Whether or not any of these come before or after pursuing a career in music is not the point. The point is to further the awareness and understanding around these topics in order to create a community that fosters mental health within the music industry.

Correlation Between Drug Addiction and Musicians

NIDA points out in their online article that there are a multitude of factors that influence addiction (2018). And "the more risk factors a person has, the greater the chance that taking drugs can lead to addiction" (2018). Biology, environment, and development are cited as the main reasons a person will become addicted to drugs (2018).

In music, "every local performer who've ever played music for a short period of time will confess that it's easy to find musicians who are high, drunk, or strung out… [and] finding musicians using hard drugs is so common that it might as well be a cliché" (Peters 2017). These environmental factors that musicians face, make the drug addiction percentages in this career path not very surprising. Peters furthers the NIDA list of factors influencing drug abuse: environment, wealth, party atmosphere, dealer benefits, permissiveness, youth, peer pressure, life on the road, drugs for creativity and performance enhancement, more dopamine for musicians, and genetic predisposition. Peters also points out that "aside from the economical and psychological reasons for using drugs as a musician, there are also legal, cultural, and social challenges linked towards music and drug use" (2017).

The accepted environment and development of the music industry does not bode well for musicians who already have a genetic predisposition to addiction. Nor are there many alternatives for musicians to seek out venues and career paths that involve clean lifestyles. Unfortunately, drug addiction negatively affects mental health, and the nature of this addiction can create long lasting damage to brain function (American Psychiatric Association 2020). Understanding and awareness of this information should encourage the music community to make some changes to what lifestyles are celebrated and available to those seeking to protect their mental health.

Impact of Drug Addiction on Mental Health

Abusing drugs negatively impacts mental health. "Brain imaging studies show changes in the areas of the brain [due to substance abuse] that relate to judgment, decision making, learning, memory, and behavioural control" (American Psychiatric Association 2020). These factors can inhibit success in the music industry as making a living as a musician needs focus, hard work, discipline, and determination. And in addition to the negative impact on mental health, "drug use is [also] one of the leading causes of preventable illnesses and premature death nationwide" (2020). It's also interesting to note the cyclical nature of a person with a mental disorder, which Chapter 1 covered in musicians, and the implications of dealing with an addiction:

"In co-occurring disorders, both the mental health issue and the drug or alcohol addiction have their own unique symptoms that may get in the way of your ability to function at work or school, maintain a stable home life, handle life's difficulties, and relate to others. To make the situation more complicated, the co-occurring disorders also affect each other. When a mental health problem goes untreated, the substance abuse problem usually gets worse. And when alcohol or drug abuse increases, mental health problems usually increase too" (American Psychiatric Association 2020).

Case Studies

The following musicians and their struggles with drug addiction do not reflect the glamorized lifestyle often portrayed in the media. A common theme is that these struggles happened behind closed doors and, more often than not, resulted in death or lifelong disease. Only female musicians are represented in this chapter.

Britney Spears: "has endlessly relapsed on drugs and even shaved her head to hide the evidence of her amphetamine addiction" (American Addiction Centres Editorial Staff 2021).

Whitney Houston: "was repeatedly in and out of rehab. She passed away in 2012, as a result of her addiction" (American Addiction Centres Editorial Staff 2021). "She was found face down in the bathtub, with a presence of drug paraphernalia nearby" (New Start Recovery 2018).

Natalie Cole: in her autobiography, revealed her "lifelong struggle with drugs, specifically crack cocaine and heroin. Although she did enter rehab once, she was diagnosed with hepatitis C in 2008 and also struggles with kidney disease" (American Addiction Centres Editorial Staff 2021).

Yoko Ono: "has openly admitted to heroin addiction. She has even claimed that she and John Lennon were kept from receiving deadly quantities of it due to a greedy dealer" (American Addiction Centres Editorial Staff 2021).

Janis Joplin: "was another famous rock singer, but died in 1970 from a heroin overdose. She was only 27 years old, but she released a lot of great hits that are still being played today. She was one of the biggest female rock stars in her era" (New Start Recovery 2018).

Stevie Nicks:

> "The Queen of Rock and the front-woman of Fleetwood Mac is no stranger to addiction. Nicks stated that early life in the band was 'dangerous.' The amount of cocaine being consumed was very much out of control. Nick's nine-year dependence on the drug would have eventually killed her had she not heeded the warning from a doctor in 1986 that her drug use had burned a hole in her nose and that any more cocaine would most likely be fatal. Nicks's treatment for cocaine addiction was only a prelude to a far more debilitating

addiction to Klonopin, prescribed by another doctor to keep the singer off cocaine. Nicks recounts that rehabilitation from the Klonopin addiction was far worse than cocaine: Her hair fell out, and her skin would peel off" (Jenning 2017).

Courtney Love:

"And drugs go way back; her father supposedly gave her LSD at the tender young age of five, resulting in him losing all custody of his daughter. She lost her husband, Kurt Cobain, to heroin addiction (and a shotgun blast) in April 1994 and just two months later lost Kristen Pfaff, the bassist in her band Hole, to heroin as well… Love went in a tailspin over the next decade. A sizeable addiction to cocaine and prescription drugs saw her frequently arrested and in and out of rehab. Love claims to have been sober since 2007 but her life has remained somewhat troubled; in December 2009 she lost custody of her daughter… who even won a restraining order against her mother" (Margolis 2013).

Marianne Faithfull:

"Was snapped up by the Rolling Stones' manager Andrew Loog Oldham [and] was most famously Mick Jagger's girlfriend and muse… She co-wrote the tellingly titled 'Sister Morphine,' only to see the Stones wrest control of the song and release it, without crediting her, on their 1971 album Sticky Fingers. By the end of the '70s she was homeless, living in an abandoned building in London… [however,] given the opportunity to cut another album, she turned in the raw, confessional Broken English; an unflinching narrative of what it was like for a glamour model and pop star to find herself an addict living on the street, all backed by understated yet fashionable musical accompaniment" (Margolis 2013).

Faithfull has stated the difficulty of being judged by the media differently than her male counterparts who had the same lifestyle as her, but managed to maintain their credibility due to their gender (Zoladz 2021). Especially in the 1967 drug trial, "'I was slandered as the wanton woman in the fur rug,' Faithfull wrote, 'while Mick was the noble rock star on trial'… it certainly wouldn't be the last rage-inducing double standard she'd endure" (2021).

Impact on Youth and Young Musicians

Drug addiction in musicians, especially famous musicians, has a negative impact on youth and young musicians. The results are two fold: one, the influence of celebrities has a direct influence on the public, "a meta-analysis showed that following an entertainment celebrity's suicide, suicide rates in the public increased significantly" (Just et al 2016, 5). One can only "imagine the positive effects of Prince receiving a timely and adequate addiction therapy, overcoming his addiction and talking openly about his experiences" (Just et al 2016, 5). The second result is the lifestyle of established musicians dictates how young musicians entering the field should be acting. This lifestyle was discussed above in terms of musicians as a group, but also applies specifically to the next generation of musicians.

Studies from NIDA-funded research show "that prevention programs involving families, schools, communities, and the media are effective for preventing or reducing drug use and addiction... when young people view drug use as harmful, they tend to decrease their drug taking" (NIDA 2018). This creates the hope that musicians who share their experiences behind closed doors, and pursue clean lifestyles, can influence youth and young musicians to be conscious of substance use.

Concluding Thoughts

White has made a point reiterating the purposes of studying drug addiction in musicians: "although it is important not to assume causality and overstate the links between some musical genres and different types of drug use, information about preferences is useful in targeting and tailoring interventions, such as harm reduction initiatives, at music festivals" (2018). Harm reduction initiatives. This would be a great first step in providing musicians a safer environment. The environment has been cited by several articles as one of the top factors of drug addictions. If every venue, every record label company, and every profiting company were to make a commitment to providing an option for a clean environment to the musicians who work to make them money... there would be a significant decrease in substance addictions. Perhaps even providing mental health advocates and therapists on staff would follow. All of this then trickles down to the youth and young musicians coming up. It would represent a community that fosters mental health.

Chapter 4.
Suicide Rates in Musicians

Introducing the Topic

We've explored the topics of mental illnesses in musicians and how de-stigmatization is a key factor in providing support. Alcohol and drug addictions have been shown to be associated with the music industry and lifestyles. An important step to support mental health in musicians with addictions is normalizing clean environments, harm reductions at festivals, and providing mental health advocate access for working musicians. In Chapter 4 we will discuss another facet of mental health often driven by depression: suicide.

Death by suicide "is a tragedy that effects families, communities, and entire countries, and has long-lasting effects on the people left behind" (World Health Organization 2021). According to the World Health Organization (WHO), there is a link between suicide and poor mental health, especially substance use disorders and depression (2021). In addition to this, many suicides are also associated with "moments of crisis with a breakdown in the ability to deal with life stresses, such as financial problems, relationship break-up or chronic pain and illness" (2021). All these factors are things musicians often deal with. Further, in studies done by Kenny and Asher, the evidence shows that "solo performers had twice the mortality rate compared with band members" (2016). Isolation is strongly associated with suicidal behaviour, "in addition [to] experiencing conflict, disaster, violence, abuse, and loss" (World Health Organization 2021). Which means that "popular musicians as an occupational group are highly vulnerable to the vagaries of their workplaces and their inherent personal vulnerabilities" (Kenny and Asher 2016, 38). Kenny and Asher's studies have shown that "popular musicians were more likely to die from non-natural causes, and their overall mortality was twice as high as that of a comparable general population" (2016, 38). With the knowledge of why death by suicide happens, and how these factors affect musicians, there can be targeted preventative measures put in place.

Suicide Statistics

The World Health Organization estimates "that around 20% of global suicides are due to pesticide self-poisoning... [and] other common methods of suicide are hanging and firearms" (2021). A study, specifically targeting musicians and suicide rates, unequivocally showed that "popular musicians died earlier and in greater proportions from violent deaths (accident, suicide, homicide) and from liver disease compared with the general US population" (Kenny and Asher 2016, 37). Kenny and Asher go on to point out that:

> "Although the common perception is of a glamorous, free-wheeling lifestyle for this [musician] occupational group, the figures tell a very different story. Results showed that popular musicians have shortened life expectancy compared with comparable general populations. Results showed excess mortality from violent deaths (suicide, homicide, accidental death, including vehicular deaths and drug overdoses) and liver disease for each age group studied compared with population mortality patterns" (37).

One of the main factors in suicide prevention is access to means: "occupations, [like musicians, are] considered to have high suicide risks because of an easy occupational access to a method of suicide" (Roberts, Jaremin, and Lloyd 2013, 1233). However, Roberts et al go on to to argue that socio-economic forces play have also become a "major determinant of high occupational suicide rates" (1237). Musicians, due to the difficulty of success and nature of working as a contractor under limited labour laws, continue to struggle with socio-economic status as well. It's interesting to note that working in the music industry continues to check off every box laid out by Roberts and team's research into death by suicide:

> "In addition to socio-economic forces and easy access to a means of suicide, the social isolation at work and the natural selection of high-risk people to certain occupations are regarded as two other important factors in the relationship between occupation and suicide. This may partly explain the high suicide rates witnessed for occupations such as artists, actors, entertainers, [and] musicians" (2013, 1238).

Given all this information, preventative measures should not be so difficult to implement in music industry careers. However, even with the awareness and knowledge around death by suicide, the numbers do not seem to be dropping. Perhaps there are other insights to take into consideration.

Potential Preventative Measures

The World Health Organization calls for preventative strategies to be comprehensive and multi-sectoral; believing that "suicides are preventable with timely, evidence-based and often low-cost interventions" (2021). In fact, suicide is a top priority in the "WHO Mental Health Gap Action Programme, which provides evidence-based technical guidance to scale up service provision and care in countries for mental, neurological and substance use disorders" (2021).

In the music industry, comprehensive and multi-sectoral preventative strategies means that the people working should have access to proper health care and help. This should be set up by the people paying them for their services, whether it's a part of gigging at a venue, for a label or record company, or catching up the digital streaming world with better labour laws. The people making money off of musicians should be held responsible for giving the musicians access to support their well being. Roberts et al support this notion:

> "Much has been made of the importance of access to a means as a major risk factor for suicide in certain occupational groups. Access to the means of prevention may also be very important. These would include mental health promotion and suicide prevention initiatives, with improvements aimed at the availability, access and use of specialist health and social care services in contact with occupational groups... Carefully targeted suicide prevention initiatives for other occupations [is] important" (2013, 1239).

Case Studies

The majority of studies from Kenny and Asher, and articles written in the media are done on musicians who have achieved a top-selling album. Given that male musicians are more likely to gain media attention, and are unequal representatives compared to the female gendered musicians, the current studies and statistics are not wholly representative of the population of musicians (Saunders 2020). Therefore the focus of this research book continues to cite female musicians. The power of personal words and stories in the case studies bring together the focus on what the future holds, or can hold. The numbers and statistics are just supports for what the people, on an individual basis, experience.

Wendy O. Williams, 48, died by suicide, a self-inflicted gunshot would. "Williams had found it difficult to live a normal life past her peak and had been despondent for a long time" (Skanse 1998). Throughout her life, Williams was known as an advocate for her rights and self expression as a woman. The fact that Williams was charged and lost her case against the arresting officer who, "grabbed [her] in a sexually abusive way" (1998), goes to show that the contributing factors to suicide may have been magnified by Williams' gender.

Sulli, K-pop star of girl band f(x), died by suicide in 2019. She was

> "known for speaking out on mental health issues, cyberbullying and women's rights… She spoke openly about her struggles with mental health issues, cyberbullying - and even her romantic relationships, which many K-pop stars are banned from doing by their management… The 25 year old insisted women should be free to dress as she pleased, and she herself was often strongly criticized for not wearing a bra in public… Her close friends said she had been depressed before her death… Several idols have since spoken out about the need for better support for stars in the K-pop industry, and the pressures they are under… Sulli is one of the few famous and outspoken Korean figures that openly talk[ed] about feminism, mental disorders, and body positivity. A true trailblazer" (Tan and Kim 2019).

Goo Hara was admitted to a hospital after surviving a suicide attempt in May 2019, then died by suicide in October 2019. "A month after she was hospitalized, she posted on social media, threatening legal action against malicious comments, and revealed that she was suffering from depression" (Kwon and Andone 2019). Hara was a close friend of Sulli, the 25-year-old K-pop artist who died by suicide in 2019. Hara had been involved in a legal battle with an ex-boyfriend who was ultimately imprisoned for physical assault and destroying her property (2019). "The episode reignited the debate over the intense pressure of K-pop stardom, which critics say is fuelled by harsh online criticism levelled at the industry's performers" (2019).

Jill Janus died by suicide at age 43. She was a recovered alcoholic, living a life of sobriety, but still battled with her mental health. She was an "incredible vocalist, a powerful performer, and a good-natured metalhead… But her death and the mental health issues that led to it, is a stark reminder that even the most robust personas in metal might be in need of help" (Krovatin 2020). Guitarist Blake Meahl spoke about how "her bouts of bipolar disorder, schizophrenia and dissociative identity disorder had been particularly difficult" (2020) in the time before her suicide. Jill's death rallied the music community

> "to acknowledge and raise awareness for mental health issues… But the lesson her death taught the world shouldn't be forgotten, and is an important reminder that even those who come off as indestructible may be fighting their own demons, and losing. Today, we remember Jill's strength, creativity, and smile, and hopefully look to keep her fire burning in all those who might feel their own slowly going out" (2020).

Paris Jackson, not a musician herself, but someone deeply entrenched with the lifestyle the career comes with, survived her suicide attempt. At age 15,

> "drowning in depression and a drug addiction, she tried to kill herself… Before that, she had already attempted suicide… [However] the hospital had a three-strike rule, and, after that last attempt, insisted she attend a residential therapy program… [Jackson] also faced cyberbullying, and still struggles with cruel online comments… After her last suicide attempt, she spent sophomore year and half of junior year at a therapeutic school… 'It was great for me,' she says. 'I was dealing with my depression and my anxiety without any help.' Her father, she says, also struggled with depression… 'I've had self-esteem issues for a really, really long time,' says Paris, who understands her dad's plastic-surgery choices after watching online trolls dissect her appearance since she was 12." (Hiatt 2017).

Fantasia, American idol winner, survived her suicide attempt. In 2010, Fantasia attempted suicide. The singer had recently experienced a breakup and

> "though she admitted the public fallout from her presumed 'affair,' she insists that he was not the cause of her wanting to end her life… 'I think everybody feels like I tried to harm myself over a man, but you know I've been in a lot of bad relationships,' she said. 'I think that had somewhat to do with it because it was so heavy, it was brand new information, I was already going through so much. But I think

26

it was just six years of me holding all that stuff on the inside and not letting it out...I got very, very tired.'... Fantasia says she was dealing with heavy financial and emotional issues [and] that she doesn't view what happened as a 'suicide' attempt, but more so, as an attempt to 'get away' and 'get rest.' Furthermore, she [says] that she doesn't regret her decision" (Alexander 2019).

Fantasia's perspective that she doesn't want her suicide attempt labelled as a suicide goes to show that the stigma around it negatively affects mental health. Because death by suicide is much higher for people who have already attempted it once, it is imperative to reduce the stigma around labelled suicide attempts. It first of all means the youth and young people can see healthy modelled mental health behaviour in the media, but it also means the person can access the proper help they may need. The common themes of depression, socio-economic status, repeated suicide attempts, lack of support available, and cyber bullying shows the music industry has a long way to go to put the proper supports in place for musicians.

Impact on Youth and Young Musicians

In 2019, suicide was the "fourth leading cause of death among 15-29 year olds globally" (World Health Organization 2021). Repeated studies have shown that a young person growing up facing adversity, and becoming a musician, the more likely they will die from substance abuse or risk-taking (Kenny and Asher 2016). If the music industry placed a higher importance on reducing the stigma around mental health, especially on the public platform, there would be reduced numbers of suicides coming from these statistics. Celebrity musicians are in a unique place in how they can influence stigma around certain topics, like suicide. This mindset would positively impact youth and young musicians in the support they can and should have access to. Overall, a community that fosters mental health means awareness, understanding, and education - all things that start with communication. It's not about fixing people who struggle with mental health, it's about taking the barriers away that might stop someone from asking or receiving help without career or relationship reprimands.

Concluding Thoughts

This chapter will end off on a quote from the World Health Organization that accurately sums up the importance of discussing these topics:

"Stigma, particularly surrounding mental disorders and suicide, means many people thinking of taking their own life or who have attempted suicide are not seeking help and are therefore not getting the help they need. The prevention of suicide has not been adequately addressed due to a lack of awareness of suicide as a major public health problem and taboo in many societies to openly discuss it. To date, only a few countries have included suicide prevention among their health priorities and only 38 countries report having a national suicide prevention strategy. Raising community awareness and breaking down the taboo is important for countries to make progress in preventing suicide" (2021).

Chapter 5.
Imposter Syndrome in Musicians

Introducing the Topic

Imposter syndrome is something that can occur in any person, in any field. It is "the feeling that a woman or man does not deserve the success s/he has achieved, that s/he has so far been lucky, and that s/he will be uncovered as someone who does not rightfully belong" (Cooksey 2012). This can negatively affect success in one's work. It brings up the question of where and why does this feeling occur in the first place? Another article refers to imposter syndrome as a fear of evaluation, or not being able to maintain success, or not being as skilled as others in the same area (Issa-Salwe 2020). "It's thought that around 7 in 10 people experience it at some point, and in the creative industries that figure climbs to 87 per cent" (2020). That is a significant amount of stress placed on a person struggling with imposter syndrome.

Imposter syndrome also often comes hand-in-hand with other issues such as depression, low self-esteem, and anxiety, all common issues in the music industry. "Around 70 percent of people working in music report anxiety and panic attacks, while 65 per cent have experienced depression versus 15 percent of the average population" (Issa-Salwe 2020). As we saw in the previous chapter, all of these factors can lead to debilitating results, like death by suicide.

Impact of Imposter Syndrome on Mental Health

Imposter syndrome impacts mental health negatively. Symptoms include: "stress, low self-esteem, and under-performance" (Cooksey 2012, 1). Sufferers of imposter syndrome often do not apply "for scholarships or jobs because they do not think they could possibly get them. [They] may also 'self-sabotage' by not asking for help or speaking poorly about themselves" (2012, 1). These resulting factors of dealing with imposter syndrome do not reflect a community that fosters mental health. In fact, many of these factors are symptoms of larger societal problems that could be causing the problem in the first place. An article by Clance and Imes explored possible reasons high achieving women have higher rates of imposter syndrome. One major contributing factor is that "success for women is contraindicated by societal expectations and their own internalized self-evaluations" (Clance and Imes 1978, 242). And, further, it is then not surprising that women seem to "need to find explanations for their accomplishments other than their own intelligence - such as fooling other people... because of lower expectancies internalized into a self-stereotype - the societal sex-role stereotype that they are not considered competent" (1978, 242). In addition to the negative effects of imposter syndrome on a day-to-day basis, there are also long living effects due to its self-perpetuating nature: "repeated successes alone [are not] sufficient to break the cycle" of continuous discounting of abilities and continuous fears of failure (1978, 242).

For musicians, "working in the music industry often comes with high stress, demanding hours, large workloads, competitive environments and a reliance on the gig economy" (Issa-Salwe 2020). Additionally, touring musicians and their teams need to learn how to handle "the instability and stressors that comes with life on the road: loneliness, anti-social hours, strain on relationships and the presence of drugs and alcohol. Perfect conditions for self-doubt" (2020). These factors, coupled with imposter syndrome, solidify the negative impact on mental health if and when there are not supports in place to foster mental health.

Stigma of Imposter Syndrome

In addition to the struggle that comes with imposter syndrome, there is also stigma. It seems that stigma continues to be one of the larger barriers to fostering mental health in any situation. Which is even more unfortunate, because being willing to speak about mental health is one of the very first steps for a person who is looking for support for their mental health. "Slowly, people are [allowing themselves to be] more vulnerable, and as a result you're starting to see more people talking about it" (Issa-Salwe 2020). This is aiding in stigma being slowly removed from mental health issues in general (2020). There is further hope when "an organization providing mental health support to people in the music industry, [Music & You, says that] imposter syndrome isn't a new thing, but the current spotlight on it is due to the honest conversations happening around the topic" (2020).

Stigma creates a huge barrier in seeking help for something that affects mental health negatively. Clance and Imes say this about high achieving females who struggle with imposter syndrome:

> "The 'impostor' is so convinced her belief is correct that nothing could be done to change it anyway. She also believes that if she revealed her assumed unique feelings of phoniness she would meet with criticism or at least very little understanding on the part of others. It is generally her anxiety about achieving a particular goal which leads her to disclose feelings of intellectual phoniness" (1978, 245).

In another article, there is a call to the general public to become more educated about imposter syndrome (Cooksey 2012, 3). "It is useful to learn that there is a well-known and well-studied name for any self-doubt one has felt, is feeling, and/or will feel. Hopefully, it is also comforting to know that others feel this way" (2012, 3). Cooksey goes on to say that "fostering an environment where people know about imposter syndrome will also help people feel comfortable talking about it" (2012, 4).

For people, especially musicians, who are struggling with the fear of revealing their imposter syndrome feelings due to stigma, there are still strategies to deal with it. "Practicing self-care [and] self-evaluation can help fight off the looming insecurities that come with imposter syndrome – as well as not being afraid to ask questions or outsource the things your skill-set doesn't cover" (Issa-Salwe 2020).

Case Studies

Dr. Kerr learned that creative women in the arts, music, and writing "have fewer protections than most women, even in academe, which is really not a lot of protection." She noticed that women in the arts "face tremendous barriers of sexual harassment from their mentors and coaches, and flagrant discrimination against females [in the creative field]" (Henriksen and Mishra 2020, 3). The case studies that follow are focused on female musicians who have been willing to talk about their self doubts and feelings of imposter syndrome.

Theresa Abalos says about her audition for Carnegie Mellon's flute studio:

"As an ambitious 18-year-old, this audition meant everything to me. I thought I ruined it. When I got my acceptance letter in March, it seemed like a miracle. Even after I woke up from shock, telling myself this wasn't a mistake, I carried all that doubt with me — through the summer after high school, into my first flute lesson at CMU. I carried it with me for the next four years. The fear that I didn't belong in the flute studio because I wasn't good enough — known as imposter syndrome — crippled my sense of self-worth as a musician. Only in my senior year would I begin to rebuild that confidence. Recently, a fellow musician mentioned not feeling 'good enough.' To me, she was one of those prodigies destined for a dazzling career. It seemed impossible that she could doubt her worth. But it made me think, maybe I wasn't as alone as I felt in the School of Music" (Abalos 2021).

Abalos' reflections are a reminder that first of all, no human is alone in their experiences, and, second of all, that being willing to seek support can positively impact mental health.

Awkwafina is a successful actress, comedian, and rapper. In an interview she says: "[I] see so many people gunning for the same thing, waiting for their break despite how talented they are. It really makes you think, why me? Why not this other person, when she could've done better?" (Female First 2019). Awkafina's reflection embodies the discussions earlier, and one coming later, in this chapter looking at why and how high achieving, successful females struggle so much with imposter syndrome.

Jennifer Lopez says in an interview: "I'm very insecure about my voice. After being told for so many years that you're not as good as this person or that person, it beats away on your insecurities... I always wanted to be a singer and a dancer but when they start dissecting you like that, it does work away at your insecurities. You know? I'm like, 'Wow, I thought I was good at this.' It does get to you. I'm only human" (Simon 2017). Lopez makes an important point, she is only human, and we all have mental health that can be negatively or positively impacted. However, there are some distinct differences in how imposter syndrome affects females in North American society.

Female Gender Differences

The dichotomy that gets created in the societal expectations of women is that they fail no matter what: succeed at the role society has given them and fail to succeed at the career they desire to work in; or, succeed at their career and fail at the role society has given them. This is one of the underlying thought patterns of a female struggling with imposter syndrome. These social expectations put on the different genders also have taught women from a small age that their successes will not come from intellect. Which means that "women [will] tend to attribute their successes to temporary causes, such as luck or effort, in contrast to men who are much more likely to attribute their successes to the internal, stable factor of ability" (Clance and Imes 1978, 242).

An example of another symptom of imposter syndrome is based around a sense of phoniness which is used as a defence strategy. Again, this example centers around the fact that people are fearful to be found out, or to reveal their thoughts on what they're feeling. The example is "a woman who remains silent in the face of an opposing viewpoint. Consequently she is left with the impression, 'if I had revealed what I really think and believe, I might not have done well. I might have been considered unintelligent.' This prevents [her] from discovering whether or not [her] authentic views would have been evaluated as sensible, and it thus contributes to the maintenance of the impostor [syndrome]" (Clance and Imes 1978, 244).

Lastly, family dynamics play a role in increasing or decreasing stigma around imposter syndrome. A child might be told directly or indirectly about the implications of success and how to achieve it, especially if a sibling has been deemed 'the smart one,' and they the sensitive or socially adept one. Part of the child may believe the family myth, and another part may want to disprove it. "[The child] succeeds in obtaining outstanding grades, academic honours, and acclaim from teachers. [The child] feels good about their performance and hopes their family will acknowledge that they are more than just sensitive or charming" (Clance and Imes 1978, 243).

Concluding Thoughts

When a female musician says, "Sometimes I'm the youngest, sometimes I'm the only woman and sometimes I'm the only black person. Most often, I feel like the only imposter" (Issa-Salwe 2020), it shows that the music industry still has a long way to go in providing opportunities to support mental health.

Reducing stigma around mental health in general is the first step in creating a community that fosters mental health. People on the public stage who are willing to talk about their own mental health struggles and successes help to educate the public on issues they themselves might be struggling with. Imposter syndrome may come from deeper societal issues that affect females differently. And it can have long lasting solutions in changing the expectations we put on the next generation. Dr. Kerr suggests a solution through changes in our education system. "In the case of intelligent and creative women who never received the support to develop boundaries or understand the barriers, they may have 'had their wings clipped.' Thus, Dr. Kerr's work is often connected to education, in supporting change through awareness" (Henriksen and Mishra 2020, 3). Overall, imposter syndrome is prevalent in the music industry and the potential positive effects that will come out of helping people deal with it outweighs the potential negative effects if we continue to ignore it.

Chapter 6.

Female Representation in the Music Industry

Introducing the Topic

Female representation in successful music careers has never been equal to their male counterparts. A research study done from 2012 to 2018 showed that "women make up 21.7% of artists, 12.3% of songwriters, and a measly 2.1% of producers" (Jackman 2020). One statistic showed "women only accounted for 10.4% of the total Grammy nominees for the most popular categories" (2020). A Task Force was put together in 2019 to address these large discrepancies and make recommendations for how to move forward. They found that "there is also a lack of women in leadership roles, such as label executives, throughout the industry" (2019, 34). Testimony from artists given to the Task Force detailed barriers women encounter during their music careers: one was "outright discrimination when auditioning for tour spots, especially (but not exclusively) in the Christian music field, where women may not be permitted to perform or travel on tour with male band members" (2019, 34). As well as performing barriers like music festival lineups, which "are also predominantly male, with female artists rarely headlining a festival and only the most well established female artists generally performing at festivals" (2019, 34). Through all of this repeated and consistent testimony, the Task Force

"identified the following issues as existing obstacles to success: Underrepresentation of women in the music industry, particularly within the industry's technical fields. Prevalence of harassment, discrimination, and/or assault as a result of informal or isolated work environments. Restriction of airtime or participation by female artists, particularly in country music. Underrepresentation of individuals of lower socioeconomic means due to high costs of entry. Lack of equal access to resources for disabled individuals. Marginalization of certain ethnicities into particular roles or genres. Phasing out of older generation music industry female professionals" (the Task Force 2019, 34).

These significant barriers are all things that can and should be remedied. There should be no reason a female pursuing a career in the music industry should have to deal with all these extra factors that come unspoken with her job description. It has a huge impact on her mental health, and her ability to maintain mental health. And as with anything that pertains to mental health, the first step is awareness, then education, then partnership with the support of the community.

General Statistics & Impact on Mental Health

Let's take a look at some of the other statistics arising from research and studies. In 2020 "the Initiative concluded that 'women are still missing in the music industry,' with women representing less than one-third of all performers and 12.5% of songwriters across 800 songs, with women accounting for 2.6% of producers across 500 songs" (Gordon 2020). Even the year with the largest number of women artists in the 800-song sample, 2016, it was still only 28.1%; "while the lowest was 2017, at 16.8%" (2020). The study also showed that "the ratio of men to women producers is 37 to 1 for 2019, while it was 47 to 1 in 2018" (2020).

A different study showed no better numbers when looking at GRAMMY nominations in 2019:

> "women only make up 24.7 percent of the overall nominations, with an additional 2.8 per cent for female-fronted groups with mostly male members, and 8.8 per cent for duos, trios or groups with a mix of genders. In comparison, 63.3 percent of this year's nominees are men. It's a number that hasn't fluctuated too drastically over the years — last year, 24.1 percent of the overall nominees were women" (Lau 2019).

These numbers here are not increasing very quickly, and they are too low to not address. The point made here, that these numbers shouldn't be ignored, is important. A lot of progress has been made in the women's suffrage movement, but often small improvements can pull a veil over underlying issues. Improvements have been made, but there is still much to do.

The Task Force reports on technical fields as well. It is interesting to note that their research of this sub-field in the music industry moved them past nominees in the Grammys and into the field as a whole. "Only 2% of producers and 3% of engineers in popular music are women. It appears that this gender gap begins early" (the Task Force 2019, 35). This statement embodies one of the most important aspects of what needs to be changed: gender gaps beginning early and getting worse with time. By the time for university class, there are already low numbers of women in sound/audio-engineering related classes; "and, as with other male-dominated fields, this disparity can lead to unconscious or implicit bias, micro-aggression, and overt discrimination or harassment that discourage women from pursuing this line of work" (35). Many of the rebuttals as to why women technicians are less represented in their field is because of their biology and wanting to raise a family instead… Unfortunately this sentiment was repeated by a female in the music industry in an interview (Massey 2000, 296). The Task Force heard the same comments: "even women with established engineering careers reported experiencing sexism, discrimination, and other barriers to professional equality, such as being encouraged to pursue an 'easier' or more 'family-friendly' career or having their artistic decisions questioned by male colleagues and artists" (2019, 35). It should be shocking that such loaded and under-handed statements are made to women. The negative impact of these statements on mental health compounds when added to the list of mental health disorders, addictions, imposter syndrome, and dealing with the barriers that come from being a certain gender.

Reason for the Imbalance

Though women face major challenges at the entry level of their field as artists and technicians, there are also obstacles faced at the peak of their career. The studies showing statistics of the number of successful women in the music industry also explore possible reasons for the imbalance. The Task Force found that the members of the nomination committees were 74% male and 26% female (2019, 9). These are committees that are "vital to recognized [GRAMMY] awards in the music community" (9). So not only are women facing the disparities in their college classes, but if they do 'make it' in the music industry, they are also facing the fact that the voting members of important awards are also male-dominated. With these two-sided challenges closing in on women in the music industry, it is any wonder at all that any get to the point of being nominated for an award, never mind actually winning it.

We've already explored the harassment and discrimination that women in the music industry are up against. However, the Task Force also learned that the music industry "often operates in ways that exacerbate the risks for many artists, performers, and workers" (2019, 37). This can be problematic when the workplace is already informal, when alcohol and drugs are often present, when studio sessions go late in isolated environments, when touring involves long hours away from family and friends and mental health supports, and especially when "the lines between work and play become blurred" (37). These problematic factors become worse when the lack of females in the music industry "means that a female performer, engineer, or songwriter may be the only woman present in these settings" (37). It is not a surprise given these uncontrolled conditions that women have reported being "harassed and/or physically assaulted late at night, in recording studios essentially monitored and controlled by nobody, where there appear to be no workplace conduct rules enforced" (37). The Task Forces points out that the federal employment laws do not apply to independent contractors or freelancers, which generally describes the people working in a studio. "Under federal employment law and the laws of many states, non-employees are not subject to the protections or the prohibitions of harassment or discrimination law" (37). The Task Force makes a comment in their report that resonates with the fact that we do not have to wait to create a better environment for anyone working in the music industry: "studios, tour sponsors, artists, others with power and influence in the industry, do not have to wait for legal changes to require creating workplaces that are safe for all" (37).

Another article explored the possible reason for the imbalance between female and male representation in the music industry. They based their research on interviews with female songwriters and producers. Their findings were less than ideal. "Over 40 percent of respondents admitted their colleagues dismissed or discounted their work or skills. Meanwhile, 39 percent have experienced stereotyping and sexualization" (Kelley 2019). The results of this research led to this conclusion: "the experiences of [these] women reveal that the biggest barrier they face is the way the music industry thinks about women" (2019). None of the reasons for the imbalance we have explored have anything to do with biology, or that women don't want to pursue a difficult career, or that there is a lack of women with talent available to work in this industry.. The barriers are based around the general perception of women. And that perception "is highly stereotypical, sexualized, and [thinking females are] without skill. Until those core beliefs are altered, women will continue to face a roadblock as they navigate their careers" (2019).

Another rather disturbing reason for the imbalance is the unwritten rules at radio stations: "current and former radio station employees stat[ed] that they had been instructed to only play a certain number of female artists or songwriters an hour, and not to play songs performed by women back-to-back" (the Task Force 2019, 39). The underrepresentation of women in the music industry stretches from performing artist to studio musician to audio engineer to producer, as well as on radio airtime and streaming services (39).

In the following case study section, we will focus on females who have been able to be successful, what they are doing for the next generation, and the barriers they have been able to break down despite all that is against females in the music industry.

Case Studies

This article listed many females in the music industry who are working hard to be successful despite the barriers. They are paving the way for others to follow suit. The more we celebrate these successes, the more the perception of females in the music industry will change for the better. Rap group the Sorority leaned into a feminist future for hip hop, "Charlotte Day Wilson helming her own project by co-producing and co-engineering her Stone Woman EP, Céline Dion re-entering the soundtrack arena [in] Deadpool 2... [and] producer Wondagurl landing some big tracks on rapper Travis Scott's chart-topping 2018 album, Astroworld" (Lau 2019). In addition to this, Metric, Ralph, Alice Glass, Dilly Dally, Partner, the Weather Station, Marie Davidson and U.S. Girls, also released some notable work (2019).

TT the Artist, founder of all-girl label Club Queen Records, says: "it's about making your own opportunities when others won't give you any" (Jackman 2020). She talks about the freedom in succeeding in a society "that tries to suppress women's creativity, sexual freedom, narratives, and identity" (2020). Her all-girl label is one way to start to "break a life of silence" (2020). TT the Artist refuses to let the barriers females face in the music industry stop her from succeeding anyways, and giving a helping hand to those coming up as well. Jackman says in his article showcasing TT the Artist: "for women to be heard in an industry overpowered by traditional norms, [starting their own labels] is a momentous step forward. ... control is one of the main advantages. This is what women have been lacking in an industry that's still an exclusive boys' club" (2020).

Deborah Dugan, former CEO of the Grammys alleged that she was "removed after complaining about sexual harassment and pay disparities and for calling out conflicts of interest in the nomination process for music's most prestigious awards" (The Associated Press 2020). The complaint included that Dugan "was paid less than former academy CEO Neil Portnow... [and] that she was also subject to retaliation for refusing to hire Portnow as a consultant" (2020). Dugan being treated this way is a poor precedent to set for other high achieving females who could risk their careers if they complain about sexual harassment, or pay disparities, or making decisions based on their own professional opinions. Dugan did not want to have Portnow as a consultant because he "had been criticized for saying women need to 'step up' when asked backstage at the 2018 show why only two female acts won awards during the live telecast" (2020). Although Dugan is not a musician, she still worked in the music industry and faces the same barriers as other females in the music industry.

Ella Fitzgerald is another female musician who broke down barriers. "She won 13 Grammys, recorded more than 200 albums, and was a regular on The Ed Sullivan Show and The Tonight Show" (Berkman 2021). Fitzgerald was also the first black woman to win a Grammy award. She did this during the Job Crow era and "fought relentlessly against discrimination as a Black female artist" (2021). She is a testament to what females can accomplish, and that their strength and talent is not to be ignored.

Madonna is yet another female figure that became a pop icon despite barriers. She was "Influenced by Debbie Harry [another female trailblazer]... Madonna has openly talked about religion, sex, feminism, and age, and remains one of the most popular artists in the world" (Berkman 2021). The strong females that influenced Madonna drives home the point that what females are currently doing, especially females in the public eye, can and do have an impact on future females. Seeing successful women in the music industry creates the impression that others can also pursue that path. The more we can strengthen this cycle, the more likely we'll be able to balance the imbalance in an organic way. However, this means that females in the music industry have to be willing to break down barriers, be vocal about their journey, and deal with the repercussions that come from breaking moulds.

Queen Latifah "was among the first women in hip-hop to win a Grammy, the same year Salt-N-Pepa won its first Grammy. Her powerful lyrics dove into topics like women's rights and urban struggles, and Latifah seamlessly navigate between rap and R&B" (Berkman 2021).

Sophia Chang, artist manager, A&R guru, and multiple record label general manager, is an Asian-American woman who never backed down. She has "been an outspoken proponent of diversity and inclusivity. Chang's memoir details her barrier-breaking career" (Berkman 2021). She says:

> "Number one is to crack open the world's imagination of what you and I could be because the world's imagination about what you and I can be is very narrow—frankly, as is our parent's generation. I just want people to say, 'Oh, okay. So an Asian-Canadian, or an Asian-American woman, could be something that I had never imagined.' And that, I think, is the most important impact that I can have in terms of our people" (Lo 2019).

Lil' Kim and Foxy Brown, female rappers, went against the preconceived image of a female rapper in the 90s. "In a genre where male artists constantly were degrading women and bragging about sexual prowess, Lil' Kim and Foxy Brown turned the tables and put women on top of the power dynamic in their music. They've influenced scores of artists including Cardi B and Nicki Minaj" (Berkman 2021). Again, we're seeing the positive after effects of what pushing through can do for the next generation.

Shania Twain, a country star, "set the stage for future acts like Taylor Swift. Her videos flipped the usual script of male rock stars backed by female dancers, centering on powerful female voices in front of male backers" (Berkman 2021).

Taylor Swift is an advocate of social justice and women's rights. "Musically, she took a bold stand when her masters were sold, calling out the hypocrisy of artists' not being able to own their own work, and planned to re-record her early songs to regain control of her narrative" (Berkman 2021).

All of these females faced barriers in their careers. Many of them decided to push forwards to success despite them. The power of influence on the next generation is showcased in many of their stories. As with any other factor that influences mental health, awareness and understanding is vital in making positive changes.

Impact on Youth and Young Musicians

The impact of current female musicians working in the music industry on youth and young musicians has already been discussed to some degree. The more that youth see balance in the music industry, and the more they hear about others' success stories, the more that will equal out opportunities for musicians coming up in the field. Female musicians seeing successful female musicians and male musicians accepting successful female musicians as a normal part of the industry helps to correct implicit bias and reduces the subtle sexism that occurs due to the imbalance of male to female musicians.

In the 2019 Juno Awards, the women in music being represented "will be encouraging for up-and-coming acts" (Lau 2019). The host for 2019 was Sarah McLachlan, "who is this iconic woman who's had this incredible career; this is inspiring for a lot of young women out there" (2019).

Another inspiring initiative for youth and young musicians is the hashtag 'WomenInTheMix,' which "called for any entity or individual responsible for or involved in the selecting and hiring of producers and engineers to commit to making hiring decisions only after considering a slate of candidates that includes at least two women" (the Task Force 2019, 16). This is not affirmative action or diversity-oriented programs, which can adversely affect the participants, it is the first steps to create awareness around women candidates and to accept them based on their merit. WomenInTheMix "also asked working producers to take gender diversity challenges in music's technical fields into account when determining who to mentor and prepare for development and advancement opportunities" (16). Part of this initiative and the resources provided by other similar organizations like She is The Music and Women's Audio Mission compiled into a website that supported "the process of identifying working female producers and engineers" (16). It is reassuring to see that the initiative was supported by the music community.

> "Over 650 artists, producers, labels, agencies, management, including Justin Bieber, Cardi B, Common, Andra Day, Ariana Grande, Lady Gaga, Emily King, John Legend, Shawn Mendes, Nicki Minaj, Katy Perry, P!NK, Post Malone, Taylor Swift, Carrie Underwood, Keith Urban, and Sharon Van Etten, signed on to the initiative and signalled their commitment to diversity and overcoming long standing barriers to success in the music industry" (16).

Concluding Thoughts

Overall we have explored statistics of females in the music industry, and reasons why this imbalance exists. There have been calls on the people with power in the industry to demand safer, more inclusive, and more diverse workplaces. We've discussed the effects of the imbalance on mental health, and the personal experiences of individuals working in the music community, which reflect what the statistics are showing. Finally, we tied in the importance of awareness and understanding on the youth and young musicians of the next generation. The Task Force makes an important point that

> "fully addressing these issues requires constant attention and effort and sustained work over many years. Achieving fully diverse and inclusive organizations means not only addressing obvious instances of discrimination or lack of full inclusion, it also means doing the hard work of facing and overcoming unconscious bias throughout the [music industry at every level]" (2019, 14).

There have been changes, and we have moved forward, but there is still a lot of work to do. Work that needs to be done by men and women alike. Work that can be done by people inside the music industry as well as outside the music industry. For it takes both a performer and a listener to make music, and we must all work together to create a community that fosters mental health from every aspect imaginable.

Chapter 7.
Music Performance Anxiety

Introducing the Topic

In previous chapters, we have discussed mental health in musicians through various topics like mental illnesses, addictions, suicide, imposter syndrome, and female representation in the music industry. The topic for Chapter 7 is something that most musicians go through to some degree. Some more than others. Many humans can relate to the feeling of stage fright, but not everyone can understand the intense feelings of performance anxiety. When something is labelled as anxiety, there is more going on than what might otherwise be in someone's control. This is an important distinction to make. It is this awareness and understanding that can help de-stigmatize identifying and asking and receiving help for performance anxiety when it gets to a point of affecting careers.

The lyrics in 'Stage Fright' by The Band (1970) adeptly captures the essence of how performance anxiety affects people on the stage, yet how musicians are expected to just push through and continue working:

"See the man with the stage fright
Standin' up there to give it all his might
He got caught in the spotlight
And when he gets to the end
He wanna start all over again
Now deep in the heart of a lonely kid
Suffered so much for what he did
They gave this cowboy his fortune and fame
Since that day, he 'ain't b'in the same

I got fire water on my breath
And the doctor warned me I might catch my death
Said you can make it in your disguise
Just never show the fear that's in your eyes
And as he says that easy phrase
Take him at his word
And for the price that the poor boy pays
He gets to sing just like a bird
Your brow is sweating and your mouth gets dry
Fancy people go drifting by
The moment of truth is right at hand
Just one more nightmare you can stand."

These powerful words tell the listener about the struggle between being famous on the stage, fighting the fear on the stage; using substances to medicate the fear, and paying the price to be able to do what a musician loves.

An article begins by asking a very good question: "It affects 75 percent of musicians, contributes to drug addiction and alcoholism, and can end careers, why aren't more people talking about performance anxiety?" (Ewens 2016). An accepted definition of performance anxiety is "the experience of persisting, distressful apprehension about and/or actual impairment of performance skills in a public context, to a degree unwarranted given the individual's musical aptitude, training, and level of preparation" (Fehm and Schmidt 2004, 99). This is one of the most frustrating aspects of performance anxiety, the fact that it can affect performance even with the correct amount of skill and preparation. The resulting effect on mental health can then be debilitating. In addition to this, exposure therapy won't change anything, "mere exposure to public performance does not automatically lead to a decrease in anxiety" (2004, 107). It is important to understand that performance anxiety, though frustrating, is not an irrational reaction to being on a stage. "It's not a natural thing to do; going out and dealing with such high levels of stress in public, and it's nothing to do with age or inexperience. No matter how highly skilled a person is, the body's pre-programmed stress responses mean they can enter a different physical state, and sometimes even a different psychological state" (Ewens 2016). However, given all of this, performance anxiety still has a stigma, and is often discounted as stage fright, and something to 'push through.' Calling performance anxiety stage fright underestimates the experience. And because "performance anxiety [isn't] well established as a psychological condition... and not very well understood," it makes it even harder to bring awareness and understanding around the condition (Ewens 2016). It's interesting to note that studies have also shown that "females are two to three times more likely to experience anxiety than males and this relationship appears to hold for music performance anxiety" (Kenny and Osborne 2006, 103). This is in line with the previous chapter on the differences between males and females in the music industry. One possible connection could also be drawn to the conclusions made in Chapter 5 on imposter syndrome.

One of the articles points out that there are not a lot of studies around performance anxiety. A possible reason for this might be that "the anxiety is being self-medicated by musicians and enabled by the industry" (Ewens 2016). Which is not unreasonable as successful careers in the music industry do not leave room for anxiety. "When your livelihood and reputation depend so heavily on performing, and thousands of breathless fans are expecting you to blow them away, feeling anxious can be seriously problematic," even if you are wildly popular (McIntosh 2016).

Effect on Mental Health

One of the trickier things about performance anxiety is that it seems to exist under a cloak of invisibility. The audience often isn't even aware when a performer is experiencing performance anxiety if the performance itself seems to be going well. But the truth is, "performance anxiety can affect any musician, regardless of how confident they may appear to the outside world" (Ewens 2016). Symptoms can be "a racing heart, dry mouth, throwing up, or a loss of appetite for hours or days before a show. It can mean getting up on stage and being completely paralyzed, or losing the ability to sing altogether" (2016). One musician says, "these days, he doesn't drink on tour to try and keep a handle on his anxiety, because while alcohol might feel helpful in the immediate short term, the after effects often work to fuel mental health problems" (2016). The negative affects performance anxiety has on mental health are multi-faceted. There are the problems that arise when it starts to influence the capacity of a musician to perform; then there are the problems that arise when the physical symptoms create unhealthy physical environments; and then there are the problems that arise when medications, whether doctor or self prescribed, cause deeper entrenched negative mental health issues.

Long Term Effects

Self medication often involves substances that end up having long term negative effects, "it's no secret that drink and drugs are often considered socially acceptable, and sometimes actively encouraged in the music industry, therefore they can easily become a crutch" (Ewens 2016). We have explored the potential outcomes of becoming dependent on alcohol and drugs in the music industry in Chapters 2 and 3. Not only does performance anxiety come with its own list of mental and physical struggles, but it is also associated with deepening the connection with addictive substances.

The physical symptoms of performance anxiety can in turn cause negative effects on overall physical health. During a high risk situation like a public performance, the two hormones adrenaline and noradrenaline are released into the bloodstream. At high levels, these can cause a faster heart rate, muscle tremors, and nausea. There are two general ways people are hardwired to react to this phenomenon. "When you harness the power of this imbalance, it can lead to a heightened state of awareness and a confident, power-packed performance. But for some people, it can lead to anxiety, memory loss or a panic attack, which often perpetuates long term anxiety" (Ewens 2016). Between the physical symptoms, the current solution of self-medication, and the cyclical nature of anxiety, performance anxiety is absolutely a topic to be aware about, understand better, and provide mental health support for those seeking it.

"Coping with the impairing condition of performance anxiety is crucial for the career, and professional musicians frequently indicate the use of drugs as a coping strategy" (Fehm and Schmidt 2004, 100). However, strategies need to be long term, and accessible by all musicians. There should be healthy strategies taught and in place for dealing with performance anxiety instead of allowing drugs and alcohol to be an acceptable strategy. These strategies also need to be activities that are used to "cope with performance anxiety in the long run, [and can] include relaxation strategies, practicing strategies, talking to different groups of people and professional counselling or therapy" (2004, 105). One article talks about the use of CBT and hypnotherapy, in addition to meditation, exercise, and relaxation. However, it also says "there is no quick fix for performance anxiety, and it's often more about maintenance and keeping stress to a minimum" (Ewens 2016). And there are councillors who will do "sessions over Skype [to] reach musicians while they're on tour in hotel rooms" (2016). This is an excellent relationship for a musician to have in the digital age, as they will have access to support no matter where they are in the world, especially given the isolating nature of being on tour in the first place.

Recognizing performance anxiety as a problem that can be worked on is a big step for many musicians. That performance anxiety is just "some inherent fault… and fighting the tendency to rely on drugs and alcohol to fix it is the first step towards tackling the problem" (Ewens 2016). This is yet another mental health aspect that relies on people, especially people in the public eye, sharing their stories. Even if it helps set up the next generation with a music industry that accepts and encourages mental health awareness and understanding, and places an importance on access to support as needed.

Case Studies

The case studies around performance anxiety in the music industry are fairly limited, and they do not match the statistics. This shows that the stigma around this kind of struggle is preventing musicians from being open about it in their personal stories. Many of the females cited below have tried the self-medicating approach, and others have tapped into healthier strategies in coping with performance anxieties.

Jess Weiss from Brighton band Fear Of Men says "there's a level of drinking you do before going onstage to feel more comfortable, but then you're kind of losing touch with what's actually happening… and if you're doing that every night, these things add up, and people can have problems before they even realize it" (Ewens 2016).

Laura-Mary Carter of Blood Red Shoes has had performance anxiety since the start of her career, but there were silver linings to take from her battle that leaked into other areas of her life. She says,

> "People would say that I was really quiet compared to my bandmate. I was thinking about it on stage, and thinking I wasn't being a certain way. I think there were moments where I got really depressed about it, but I remember on tour every show I came off and would be really annoyed at myself, and just think that I was rubbish. More than often before a show, I'm still pretty much shaking. I'll have to talk myself around… [But] I think I   probably have that anxiety in other areas of life were I not to be in a band. Working through this has helped me overcome certain things and that confidence has spread throughout my life and now I say yes to more. I welcome what scares me" (Ewens 2016).

48

Another benefit to celebrities talking about their performance anxieties is that "it puts a name to a condition that somebody might have been living with for quite some time but didn't know that it was a recognized medical condition" (McIntosh 2016). And we've already discussed the impact of publicizing personal celebrity stories has on the general public.

Impact on Youth and Young Musicians

Other than to set up youth and young musicians with a community that fosters mental health through awareness and understanding, it is also important to be aware that some problems, like alcohol dependency as discussed in Chapter 2, are detrimental starting at a much younger age. Performance anxiety can be severe enough to end careers because it can induce depression and panic. There should be more education around how to support people who struggle with it when it first starts happening. Our society can discount a lot of mental health struggles until it impacts careers in adulthood, but often these struggles begin much much sooner, and can be better supported if intervention happens much much sooner. One possible source for the type of performance anxiety that induces total depression or "sheer sickening panic, [is] the quality of the attachment relationship they had with their parents" (Ewens 2016). An anxious and insecure attachment results in "feeling more overwhelmed, humiliated and ashamed by a performance or the prospect of one. The anxieties arising around [the performances] trigger earlier shaming experiences" (2016). This source is directly related to youth and young musicians as their performance anxiety would begin as soon as this type of relationship was established. It is also possible "that students reject or are uncertain of a career as a professional musician because of the discomfort associated with high music performance anxiety" (Kenny and Osborne 2006, 107). This is why studying performance anxiety in young musicians is just as important as recognizing it in adult performers. "Many children display similar constellations of physiological symptoms of music performance anxiety as adult musicians and that performance anxiety was negatively correlated with self-esteem and performance quality" (104). Given all this data around when performance anxiety begins in addition to the negative effects, more studies and long term treatment plans are needed "to determine how best to assist young musicians whose performance and career prospects are impaired by this disabling condition" (110).

Music performance anxiety is most likely to surface when other anxieties are present, and by the gender of the performer. This is why it is important to understand the discrepancies between female and male artists as we continue to look towards equal opportunities in the music field. "Females reported more emotional distress than males and had significantly higher total scores. These findings confirm patterns found in adult performers and across other forms of performance anxiety in children" (Kenny and Osborne 2006, 109). However, past negative experiences trump both of these indicators if negative experiences become a factor. Which is another reason to understand the pressures we put on young musicians as they gain experience in the music industry.

One more important note to make is that there are significantly lower rates of drug usage among the young musicians samples studied. So then, the increased drug use can be correlated with musicians as they become entrenched in the music industry. This also means that preventative measures would be more effective if they were targeting the younger generation of musicians, because "nearly half of the students impaired by performance anxiety and still about one third of the unimpaired ones would accept taking prescribed drugs if necessary to cope with performance anxiety" (Fehm and Schmidt 2004, 101). Other strategies that student musicians cited were Alexander technique, hypnosis, massages, yoga, positive self-instruction, relaxation techniques, and special practicing techniques. However, there isn't a lot of data available on coping strategies for adolescent musicians, and so the strategies recommended are based on an individual basis.

Concluding Thoughts

Performance anxiety isn't just stage fright. It is an involuntary physiological and mental response to a public performance. Many musicians struggle with it, and often turn to harmful substances as a strategy to deal with it, as their careers depend on successful performances that performance anxiety can hinder. These types of coping strategies can have negative long-term effects, like addictions and other mental illnesses. The young generation of musicians "called for more support either from their teachers or from outside of school to cope with their anxiety" (Fehm and Schmidt 2004, 98). There is a need and a want for mental health supports to be in place, especially for youth and young musicians. The music industry does not have to wait for labour laws to catch up to protect contract workers. Bringing awareness and understanding to these mental health issues can help de-stigmatize the issues, and be the first step for what environments are acceptable for musicians to work in.

"There's a lot of pressure on people in modern life, and [the] idea that we have to present this perfect picture of ourselves is taking something away from the authenticity of being a human being…. It's important to make mistakes, and it's important to tell people if you feel sad or if you feel low, and I think it can be all too easy to present this image of someone that is super happy and everything is perfect" (McIntosh 2016).

This quote sums up the call to the community to foster mental health through taking down the barriers that stigma creates. Mental health isn't a thing to be fixed, but instead an aspect of a human being that should be respected. The lovely spectrum that we all live on with our uniqueness, but also certain similarities, is beautiful, and we should each have choices available to influence our mental health, just as we have choices available to influence our physical health.

Chapter 8.

Social Influences on Musical Preference

Introducing the Topic

We have been taking a deep dive into the mental health of the music industry as a whole. Many topics have been represented through academic studies, through individual reporting, and through possible impacts. The topic for Chapter 8 is another challenging topic to dissect because much of the impact stems from intangible factors. Social influences on musical preference is an important topic to understand because it showcases how the group influence can impact ownership over identity.

Music preference is an intimate thing. It becomes part of one's identity. There are studies that have asked the question of whether music preference is tied to gender, or personality. And other studies that wonder what came first in that potential correlation: music preference or identity? One thing is for sure, "we take it for granted that the music we like and listen to says something important about us and [we] make judgements about others based on their musical tastes" (Carlson et al 2017, 3). It seems there are many influences on musical preference, social aspects being one of them. The social influences on musical preference is important to understand because it relates to identity. And if society places boundaries on what is acceptable or not acceptable to prefer, it absolutely affects mental health and retains the ability to be expressive.

Music is extremely accessible in our modern world. From streaming services to radio, to retail playlists, to local live shows, it permeates every single thing we do. "The average American citizen is exposed to up to six hours of music each day. There is an entire industry focused on using music to influence people" (Phelps 2014, 100). In terms of musical preference, there may be more manipulation than we'd like to admit. The psychological studies that have gone into streaming services and retail playlists are extensive. Then there is the media influence on musical preference. The media influence on musical preferences does not stop at just the type of music, but also the type of people advocating the preference. Representation in the media has strong correlations with what the public will prefer, but also what they will accept as preferences by different groups of people. One example we will explore is females in the heavy metal genre of music.

Though the field of music preference is a complex area of study because preferences are unique to each individual, it is still important to have an awareness and understanding around it when fostering mental health is the goal, because identity and how identities are formed absolutely affect mental health. Music is intricately entwined with identity. Self-reflection and self-efficacy can be traced to development of identity. Understanding where music preference comes from can help us understand ourselves. Knowing the influence that authority figures and peers have can bring attention to knowing where identity is formed. It is especially important when the whole point of this book is to discover what it will take to build and maintain a community that fosters mental health in the music industry. To help shape the identity of the music industry as a whole. To break down barriers that might prevent a person from pursuing a career in the music industry. To create spaces that performers, tour crews, venue owners, listeners, and everyone involved in musicking (Small 1997) can all feel safe in, and all have access to support as needed.

Another integral aspect of musical preference is the teacher's role in the development of the student. There is "a strong correlation between occupational identity and socialization influences in pre-service music teachers. More specifically, parents, teachers, and private lesson instructors were the main source of motivation in participants' decisions to pursue a career in music education" (Phelps 2014, 28). An individual in our society is always part of a larger group. And that group will have an identity that will influence the individual. Further, "group identity, whether it is that of a religious group, peer group, or cultural group is a fundamental aspect of how we individually identify ourselves, and music is a strong force within the formation of a group's identity" (Phelps 2014, 28). This is important to understand because it means that your own preferences were not chosen as an individual, but rather from the influence of the group. This is not to say your identity is a lie, but it should rather be grounds for self-reflection on why you like the things you do. And, further, to encourage exploration of things you may have thought you didn't like, because it is unlikely you deviated, as "a person that identifies with a certain group most likely immerses completely in the style, ideology, and culture of that group" (28).

Lastly, there is also referential meaning to explore in how it affects musical preference. Referential meaning in music is mostly referring to the lyrics in music, and what those lyrics represent. Lyrics were found to be an influential aspect of musical preference. "Although often thought of as a positive aspect of music, Referential Meaning can be negative for many listeners. For example, a piece of music with offensive lyrics to a certain population of people may be played on the radio, thus alienating that population from that music or radio station" (Phelps 2014, 21). Again, we see a group identity with a certain preference making choices that separate themselves from others based on a preference that could have more to do with the group than the individual. This is an important note to make, because that separation can lead to mental health struggles and creates barriers to getting support if needed. A community that fosters mental health in the music industry is based on awareness and understanding of all factors that affect mental health. This includes awareness and understanding of musical preference and how it may be affecting individuals within a larger group mentality.

Social Influences Impacting Mental Health

Peers can influence preferences of music. This is probably due to the collective identity that is formed during formative adolescent years. The social aspect of being a human demands certain mirroring for survival. In terms of music, this may mean that if your preferences don't match your peers', you will be treated differently. However, if you force your preferences to match your peers', it may lead to a more ingrained sense of imposter syndrome which can lead to other declines in mental health.

One social factor that influences musical preference is social functionality. Which is basically referring to the role of the music in any given situation. The context is important to accepting different types of music in different situations, "cultural and social contexts influence preferences... the functionality of music to an individual may play an important role in determining music preference, including social functionality" (Carlson et al 2017, 19). In terms of mental health, this can be seen as a benefit if one has a music preference that is not accepted by their group, but could be accepted in context.

Gender differences can also affect musical preferences, not necessarily based on individual choices, but pressure from group mentality. Females are often not viewed as serious listeners of certain genres of music because of underrepresentation. As we explored in the chapter on gender differences in musical artists, this situation can create micro aggressions in music listeners as well. It sets up the music community to assume females are in attendance for reasons other than enjoyment of the music, like to find a romantic partner. "Not only does this devalue female involvement in music scenes, but it also reduces women to sexual objects that have no genuine interests outside attracting the heterosexual male gaze" (Roberts 2021). The impact of mental health in this situation is two-fold: one, it can increase the imposter syndrome; and two, it can deteriorate important relationships in the music community. Roberts continues on in his article to point out that many females in the music industry have had to resort to strategies to "avoid gender discrimination," such as using pseudonyms, being conscious of physical appearance, and attending shows with other female peers (2021). The negative impacts on mental health through making decisions out of fear of rejection are also present in this kind of influence on musical preference.

Importance of Education & Awareness

Musical preference is majorly influenced by familiarity: studies "found that familiarity through repetition of the music selections was the main reason participants cited for liking the music" (Phelps 2014, 22). It becomes even more concerning that radio stations are instructed not to play as many female artists, by limiting their exposure to the general public, it creates yet another barrier in getting to a successful point if their listeners cannot become familiar with female artists and build a preference for them: "results showed participants preferred musical examples that were more familiar" (Phelps 2014, 19). Being aware of this, and understanding your own choices on preference can help solidify your support of different musicians. It can help music communities grow out of genuine interest, after discovering why specific preferences exist. It can create avenues of growth and stronger relationships between people who come together through building awareness and being educated.

Another reason preferences are important to be aware of and understand is related to this study's result of how attractive male musicians affect perception compared to unattractive male musicians performing. The fact that they have created a subjective dichotomy in their study creates a problem in thinking that these are the only two options. That anything past this doesn't count in the study of preference in music. "Another aspect of charisma that significantly affects perceptions of performance quality is attractiveness. There is a lot of research that deals with this, audio-visual performance ratings of attractive males were significantly improved over those of unattractive males or audio only stimuli" (Phelps 2014, 25). Unfortunately studies like this only add to the gender discrepancies that already exist among musicians. To focus only on males in a study further proves that more needs to be done to balance out the female representation in the music industry.

One article calls on instructors and educators to provide avenues of musical exploration for students to counterbalance group mentalities that start to become ingrained at a young age. "In order to provide appropriate musical stimuli that can expand students' preferences, educators need to apply the information regarding the effect of age and the development of preferences that numerous studies have found to instruction" (Phelps 2014, 55). However, this could potentially be problematic if the instructors themselves have deep seated preferences that come from past group mentalities and haven't done the growth to move past, or at least realize and take ownership over their preferences.

Case Studies

Nikki Roberts, blogger, metal enthusiast: "however, this pair of men believed that I couldn't be interested in metal music without the influence of a boyfriend they assumed I must have" (Roberts 2021).

Amanda Flores, Chicago musician, believes "her identity is exploited by promoters and that she is often reduced to nothing but her gender and sexuality by males who book her bands [and] also expressed that many men use her status as a woman against her. She said she has received many remarks from men who doubt her abilities as a musician simply because she is female" (Roberts 2021).

Roger Phelps: this story shows positive influences that shaped music preference in a way that lined up with his values and interests. Compared to the other case studies where a person was genuinely interested in a type of music, but was prevented or ridiculed in participating in that genre because it wasn't socially accepted by their peer group or authority figures in their life. This male perspective is being shown here to highlight the drastically different experience he had growing up as a male in the music industry.

"I got into the low brass room and picked up the tuba and played 'the lowest note' one can possibly play on the tuba. Or at least that is what the instructor told me. I didn't care that it wasn't actually the lowest note because I thought it was so cool that I could play the lowest notes in the band. All that being said, it was my group of friends, who were also going [to the band class] that influenced me to want to go. Those friends were in band with me through high school and are still some of the closest friends... I was at a church camp during the summer and one of the councillors at the camp brought a new recording of this band and let his group listen to it. It was awesome and I loved it. Luckily for me, maybe not so much my dad, they sold this tape at the bookstore there and we got to drive home several hours, completely immersed in the music. This greatly influenced my propensity towards rock. Another major impact from my family came in the form of my grandparents. I remember going to visit every Fourth of July. They were members of a band that would perform a couple of tunes including the 'Star Spangled Banner' in front of thousands of people in a park before a huge fireworks display took over the sky. I remember the long years of learning an instrument and waiting until the day I was finally old enough to play with them in the community band. The experiences of exposure through family are some of the most powerful and although these may be far out of a person's mind when they make a choice about what song to listen to, they have greatly impacted their preferences" (Phelps 2014, 31).

This anecdote seems innocent enough. However, when you take into account that every preference the author has at a young age that was supported by his peer group and family was never contested, it seems like he was never encouraged to explore different types of music, nor was he ever challenged on why he was choosing certain genres (male camp counselor, father figure, male instructor)... had it been a female, or an individual coming from a different group mentality, these preferences might not have held up through adolescence. It is interesting to note that both his grandparents play in the community band, in seemingly equal roles, and this is a concept we will explore Chapters 9 and 10 as a way forward.

Impact on Youth and Young Musicians

In education, teachers have been trained to influence their students' preferences as a ploy to get them to stay in their music programs for longer. This unfortunately puts the teacher in a place of authoritative opinions and doesn't necessarily allow for deviation in student innate preferences and could perhaps lead to imposter syndrome, or valuing one type of opinion (authority) over another (student). This is a thought process that inhibits exploration and creativity in music for fear of rejection. It possibly sets up the authority to only classify certain successful musicians as 'real music' and discounts any that are less than perfect. Which would in the long run affect a student from pursuing or participating in music due to the comparison that gets up through this relationship. "The majority of students cited the enjoyment of the music as the major reason for staying in band and by understanding how to sculpt preferences, educators can provide an enjoyable and meaningful time for all of their students" (Phelps 2014, 14). On the surface, this is not necessarily a bad thing, as there can be well rounded educators with the best interests of their students in mind. However, in the name of being aware how and when this happens, it can keep one's own self-reflection grounded. One researcher even uses "preference research to outline important areas in music education that can be controlled by the educator" (14). And though the premise of this would be to expand the variety of music that students are exposed to, it can also have a limiting effect. The researcher continues on to say "understanding their students' preferences [would] make it easier to get students into music programs and to stay in music programs" (14). However, we are again left with the potential that this manipulation is solidifying the current accepted preferences by the society, and not encouraging innate preferences.

In viewing the educator role in a more positive light, is to see the importance of the music teacher helping increase exposure to different types of music. Because "once students enter late elementary school and middle school preferences for a variety of music decrease drastically and generally mimic those of their peers and popular culture" (Phelps 2014, 53), and the students may be bringing their limiting preferences to the classroom already. We've already discussed how an authority figure has a lot of influence over musical preferences. So how can we ensure that students are being engaged and discovering different genres of music on a journey to take ownership over their own preferences? That is why having an understanding and awareness around these issues can help educators be the role model in discovering and expanding their musical preference, and in turn, affect the way they teach the next generation. "An intimate understanding of research in the field of music preference and education [makes it] possible to provide all students with a meaningful, fulfilling, and comprehensive music education" (Phelps 2014, 15).

A last thought on the impact of musical preference on youth and young musicians are the instrument choices they accept after their parent's experiences with what is widely performed. A study found that parents selected instruments for their children based on gender. "In a masculine-feminine comparison of instruments, the flute, violin, and clarinet were rated as the most feminine instruments and the drums, trombone, and trumpet the most masculine instruments. These stereotypes tended to be supported through a social structure within the instrumental organization" (Phelps 2014, 47). This is even more evidence to call to attention biases in preferences of instruments based on gender, and preferences based on group mentality. However, it was interesting that in the study, "girls tended to be more likely to play a nonconforming gender instrument than boys. This suggests that girls may be less swayed by the instrument bias" (47). Perhaps because girls have already discovered the barriers that face them at this point, that they are used to ignoring gender bias. Whereas males might struggle to crossover into a feminine instrument due to not having as much exposure to overcoming stigma.

Concluding Thoughts

"Music has four social functions: to help with the development of a self-identity, relate public and private emotional lives, to help shape the memory of pop culture across time, and help establish a sense of commonality among members of a group" (Phelps 2014, 28). The act of making music, or "musicking" (Small 1997) is an important part of being human. It is vitally connected to relationships, "to make music is to take part in a discourse concerning relationships" (Small 1997, 9). Music is connected to the development of identity. "The influence authority figures, parents, friends, and even important religious groups have on the development of self has an equally important bearing on the development of musical preference" (Phelps 2014, 28). In building awareness and understanding about why and how you've developed preferences can influence future generations to take more ownership over their own preferences, especially if it deviates from their group's mentality. "The ability for music educators and therapists to understand how music preferences are formed for different people is vital to the success of their students and patients" (Phelps 2014, 101). All of this work continuously adds to building a community that fosters mental health through being open and accepting, and focusing on relationships.

Chapter 9.
Impact of Music on the Listener

Introducing the Topic

In the previous chapters, we explored a lot of the mental health present in the music industry from the musicians' side. In this chapter, we'll take a detour and see the effects of music on the listener's mental health. Listener includes being a musician, or part of the audience, a crew member, any person with hearing that can or does listen to music. This is another aspect of mental health in the music industry because it points to why humans engage in music, and how it essentially can improve mental health from a physical point of view, but also from a community support point of view. "Music engages many areas distributed throughout the brain, including those that are usually involved in other kinds of cognition" (Weinberger 2006). There are many theories as to the origins of music, much of which cannot be proven due to lack of tangible evidence. However, research scientists do understand a lot of what happens in the brain when it is involved in music listening or music making.

> "Musical activity involves nearly every region of the brain that we know about, and nearly every neural subsystem. Different aspects of the music are handled by different neural regions - the brain uses functional segregation for music processing, and employs a system of feature detectors whose job it is to analyze specific aspects of the musical signal, such as pitch, tempo, timbre, and so on" (Levitin 2006, 86).

Given this information, it is no wonder music has been a part of every society, all through every era that we know of. It makes sense that music plays a large role in development. Music skill and perception is something humans are born with. The goal of music is to convey "a universal truth that if successful, will continue to move and to touch people even as contexts, societies, and cultures change" (5).

Though music is well understood to be an innate part of being human, a distinction has risen over the past 500 years that has separated our western society into music performers and music listeners. It is only recently that this has occurred. "Throughout most of the world and for most of human history, music making was as natural an activity as breathing and walking, and everyone participated" (Leviton 2006, 6). In our modern times, there is an emphasis on "technique and skill, and whether a musician is 'good enough' to play for others. Music making has become a somewhat reserved activity in our culture, and the rest of us listen" (7). This unfortunate divide gives the impression that some people are musical and some people are not. This is incorrect. Every person is musical. Some people get paid to be musical because they have a desire to develop their skills in an organized way. And it is this group of people that need to still be protected under labour laws and have access to support for mental health. However, one way for our society to move forwards together is to close that gap between performers and listeners. Perhaps to look at ways to involve communities of people in music making, to lean into the idea that allowing children and youth to freely express themselves in music to aid in development, and to accept that people coming together to experience what our brains are hardwired to do is what will strengthen relationships and reduce stigma around our differences.

Impact on Understanding Mental Health

This biological information on how our brains process listening to music and participating in music making can help our understanding and therefore supporting positive mental health in the music industry as a whole. It is interesting to look at the differences between what scientists consider the 'mind' and what they consider the 'brain' and how music can marry these two ideas. "The word mind refers to that part of each of us that embodies our thoughts, hopes, desires, memories, beliefs, and experiences" (Levitin 2006, 83). Music affects the mind in that it is an art form and integrates emotions. Music conveys our thoughts, music is a representation of our experiences and cultures, and music contains many hopes, desires and memories. "The brain, on the other hand, is an organ of the body, a collection of cells and water, chemicals and blood vessels that resides in the skull" (83). Music (performing and listening) also utilizes the actual working brain in how it needs different areas of the brain in order to operate. Being a musician, and listening to music, means the brain is active in many areas. There is no other activity scientists are aware of that uses the same areas. Or the amount of areas in the brain.

In terms of mental health, understanding biological information is useful because it applies to all humans. It takes away the idea that only musicians struggle with certain things. Mental health has a lot of stigma that comes with struggling with it. Reducing stigma is a major step towards seeking and receiving support. Stigma gets reduced with awareness and understanding. Awareness and understanding begins with people coming together as a community. Knowing that all humans can participate in music making is a way to bring together people.

Importance of Music in the Community

This information helps people understand that music is for everyone, to be enjoyed and performed by everyone, not just trained professionals. Perhaps making sure music is fully integrated into every aspect of community is a way to help understand and support career musicians not feel so separated. Levitin mentions in his book that music is intricately woven into our cultures. The experience of music helps bond groups of people together. He explains this concept by first showing how music is different from other sounds in our environment:

> "Perhaps the ultimate illusion in music is the illusion of structure and form. There is nothing in a sequence of notes themselves that creates the rich emotional associations we have with music, nothing about a scale, a chord, or a chord sequence that intrinsically causes us to expect a resolution. Our ability to make sense of music depends on experience, and on neural structures that can learn and modify themselves with each new song we hear, and with each new listening to an old song. Our brains learn a kind of musical grammar that is specific to the music of our culture, just as we learn to speak the language of our culture" (2006, 108).

At the risk of driving this point home too hard, this knowledge shows that music needs to be a part of a community for that community to form group bonds and survive. The music industry is not an isolated industry, because all humans have musical abilities. It is unique in the sense that moving forwards involves re-integrating the community into musical practices. And doing this while still maintaining that some people will want to develop their skills to the point of building careers and getting paid.

Impact on Youth and Young Musicians

The positive or negative impact on youth and young musicians is determined by the level of understanding of the role music plays in their lives. "Youngsters who had received greater exposure to music in their homes showed enhanced brain auditory activity, comparable to that of unexposed kids about three years older" (Weinberger 2006). One way to break a cycle is to begin with the next generation. Education reforms and expectations can be the start of lessening the divide between performers and listeners. Youth and young musicians can be educated on mental health in the music industry starting at a more appropriate age. A more appropriate age is anytime from birth as all humans have musical abilities. Even a newborn will recognize music they started hearing in the womb 5 months into the pregnancy. The more the adult generation can apply knowledge and self-reflections to the youth today, the more benefits will be seen.

Concluding Thoughts

"The difference between music and a random disordered set of sounds has to do with the way fundamental attributes combine, and the relations that form between them" (Levitin 2006, 17). This definition of music may seem obvious to you, but we are the only species that differentiates between random sounds and sounds that have relationships to one another. "When these basic elements combine and form relationships with one another in a meaningful way, they give rise to higher-order concepts such as meter, key, melody, and harmony" (17). Overall, music exists for a reason. We may not be able to pinpoint where exactly music comes from, but we can certainly see and experience the benefits of music, both as a performer and as a listener. Both roles involve musicality and both roles point to the human as a musician. One of the important take-aways from this chapter is to realize the impact music has on our brains, and our children's brains. This should encourage everyone to participate in music in their communities and start to close the gap opened between performers and listeners, and look towards all humans as musicians. Just as all humans are born with the ability to breath, communicate, and build relationships. All humans have the ability to participate in music whether or not they are getting paid for it.

Chapter 10.
Supports for Mental Health

Introducing the Topic

After the previous nine chapters, its surprising music has continued to thrive at all. But as we've seen in the previous chapter speaking to some reasons as to why we listen to music, it would be shocking if music ever didn't thrive. This last chapter is focused on supports available in the music industry, as well as the benefit of building a supportive community. Though there is still much work to be done to de-stigmatize mental health issues, the music industry is not new to talking about it:

> "The music industry is taking action like never before to address the growing mental-health crisis. There are new initiatives popping up from both corporate giants and grassroots organizations; festivals and benefits being planned to raise awareness of mental health; and efforts by record labels and artists to de-stigmatize mental illness. Musicians from Bruce Springsteen and Justin Bieber to Lizzo and Demi Lovato are increasingly opening up about their own mental-health struggles... The idea of providingsupport to artists has been around for decades — the Recording Academy launched MusiCares to lend medical and financial help back in 1989 — but recently, the number of   resources for musicians in need exploded." (Frehsee 2020)

Leaders in the industry and artists alike are starting to share their own experiences about mental health. This is helping to raise awareness. It is vitally important to care for your mental health, however it can be tricky to get started or to know what might work for you. Mental health is an individual thing, and needs individual care. But there are organizations around that can help provide support, and there are general ways to learn about your own mental health and how to keep it in a place that you choose and have control over.

Hope For the Future

Two organizations are outlined below to show prominent organizations that are available for people in the music industry to access. This is tangible evidence that people do care, and are willing to help.

Silence the Shame Organization:

"A world leader on erasing the stigma and educating communities on mental wellness through Community Conversations, Wellness Trainings, compelling content, and outreach programs... Silence the Shame is a nonprofit organization that focuses on education and awareness around mental health. Programs and initiatives consist of Crisis Response Trainings, Community Conversations, Wellness Trainings, digital content, and outreach events. We aim to normalize the conversation, peel back the layers of shame, eliminate stigma, and provide support for mental well-being" (Silence the Shame 2021).

Backline Organization meets with their clients through a one on one conversation before matching the individual with appropriate resources. These resources include AA meetings, therapists, life coaches, and support groups. Accessing backline services is free.

"Backline is a non-profit that connects music industry professionals and their families with mental health and wellness resources. [They] want to build a safer and more supportive music industry by helping our community access quality mental health care providers that understand this line of work... Connect with a community of music industry professionals around the world. Led by licensed mental health providers, Backline support groups meet online, and provide a safe space to come together to share your experiences... Take advantage of free wellness subscriptions, curated content, and exclusive discounts to support your journey—on and off the road" (Backline 2021).

Awareness & De-Stigmatization

The more we can discuss mental health, the more normalized it will become. The struggling with it part, and the speaking about it part. "While there is evidence that we have efficacious treatments for mental illness, including psychotherapy and medication, there are barriers that exist to people getting the care they need" (Friedman 2021). One of these barriers is the stigma tied to mental health struggles. "This stigma both vilifies people with mental illness and blames them for their condition" (2021). When in fact, mental illness does not equate to automatically being a bad person, nor is it in the control of the person with the mental illness. However the idea that this is the thought process of society is incredibly harmful to people accessing the help they may need. Further, the stigma around mental health "purports that people who struggle with mental illness are not only 'crazy' and 'dangerous,' but also that they are 'lazy' and unable to overcome their mental illness because they do not work hard enough to make changes in their life" (2021). It's no wonder people who struggle with mental health don't want to talk about it, or delay getting help, or struggle building relationships. But, all of these things, talking about it, getting help, and relationships, are necessary to having a higher quality of life. "People who struggle with mental illness may face stigma and even discrimination, including health care systems that do not offer mental health care comparable to the care of other conditions" (2021). Therefore, building awareness around mental illness, being a mental health advocate, and continuing the work to de-stigmatize mental health in both the music industry as well as all industries is vital to creating a holistic community that fosters mental health.

Forwards Through Community

A community can mean many things these days. But basically it is a group of likeminded people. It can be an online support group. It can be a religious group. It can be a group of peers from a high school. It can be an adult soccer team. A community of people means a group of people who play different roles within the group, and have a common purpose. Mental health advocates in the community are extremely important. "There are many ways of combating the stigma of mental illness. But one of the most powerful forces that we have in combating the stigma of mental illness is our mental health advocates" (Friedman 2021). Mental health advocates are people who work to bring awareness to the struggles of people with mental health issues, "sometimes they are bravely sharing stories of struggling with their own mental illness or the illness of a loved one. Other times they are letting us know that if we struggle with mental illness that there are people out there who want to help rather than judge and ridicule" (2021). This is so important in order to move forwards as a community. There is power in someone being willing to share their story, or their way of getting help, or what is available for support or treatment. Whatever way mental health advocates are deciding to help, it all helps to reduce stigma around mental health, and that is the ultimate goal in someone seeking and getting the help they need should they desire it. Friedman goes on to talk about the importance of mental health advocates:

> "We need all of the mental health advocates we can get. Every time someone steps up and challenges the stigma of mental illness and supports people who suffer, it is a huge step towards tackling the mental health crisis. In recent times, one group of people to step up as mental health advocates and challenge the stigma of mental illness have been musicians" (2021).

The way forwards is through community, and though musicians are a group of people that have struggled with mental health, they are also a group that is extremely supportive, and have been using their stages to share more stories and invite their fans to come together as a community.

Impact on Youth and Young Musicians

The impact of having a supportive community on youth and young musicians is huge in terms of fostering awareness and understanding of mental health. Awareness and understanding are the first steps in giving space to a person to seek and use help and support that are available in the music industry as well as other industries. For youth and young musicians entering the music field, there are some main areas of concern that affect the rates of anxiety and depression: "money worries, poor working conditions, relationship challenges, and sexual abuse/bullying/ discrimination. Most professional musicians can identify with at least a couple of these" (Raine 2019).

Another important aspect to positively impact youth and young musicians is to encourage artists to share their stories. Sharing their experiences on a public stage can reach much further than any ad or marketing campaign to support mental health. The power in these stories being shared by artists is that it helps listeners "feel less stigmatized and alone in coping with their mental health issues" (Friedman 2021). Lessening the feelings of stigmatization and loneliness is often the role a supportive community will play, which drives home the point of using a community to help support mental health. Community built through mental health advocates, through building relationships with like minded people, through accessing supports that are available, and through being willing to listen to other people's stories and share your own.

Concluding Thoughts

In this final chapter, we've discussed that though there are many hurdles for the music industry to still overcome, there are supports available. There are people who are advocating for mental health. Perhaps the most important are the mental health advocates, who are the frontline people in creating normalcy around speaking about and getting help for mental health issues. In addition to this, mental health advocates can help people identify conditions like depression, burnout, and imposter syndrome, and companies like the Association for Electronic Music provide further information "on coping strategies for managers and artists, who tend to tour heavily" (Frehsee 2020).

> "Because just as we revere our rock stars, we also often vilify them when they struggle. Many musicians have seen how the same music industry colleagues, media, fans, or even bandmates that cheer them on can turn on them when they struggle with depression, addiction, or suicidality. They have experienced the lack of empathy and compassion that often accompanies being afflicted with mental illness" (Friedman 2021).

This quote sums up why support is important to people in the music industry. Musicians' unique position on a public stage sets them up to be able to positively influence the music industry, but at the same time, can be their downfall if they are vilified due to their struggles. Building a strong community around you seems to be the best way to gain support for yourself as well as for others. But if that is not available, there are places available that provide support for free, and online accessible. The benefits in supporting your mental health outweigh the potential negative outcomes if mental health issues are not addressed. Overall, mental health is vitally important to quality of life and is a part of every human being's experience.

Conclusion from the Author's Point of View

This entire book was written for two main purposes: one, a call to mental health advocates to continue to build supportive communities and relationships with the people around them; and two, to point out that we need to take better care of the people who work in the music industries. I have come to the conclusion that both purposes are attainable, and it starts with the willingness to be educated. And, specifically for the music industry, it starts with a community involvement in musical activities. Both education and musical participation require openness. Openness to other people's experiences, and openness to new experiences. Music has the power to transform people's lives. The raw emotion that listeners experience in music is a link to the raw emotions that musicians put into their work. "It is perhaps because musicians have often struggled with their mental health, endured stressful times, experienced the stigma of mental illness, and yet were still able to deliver powerful and life-changing music that they have something from their fans that is invaluable in combating the stigma of mental illness - trust" (Friedman 2021). Music has been the soundtrack of our lives. Music has been present during the good times and the bad times. Music has the power to transform, to communicate, and to bridge people together. I hope that in reading this book, you have been able to relate to the stories, the statistics, and the importance of what we need to do moving forwards as a community that fosters mental health.

Works Cited

Abalos, Theresa. 2021. "12 classical musicians on imposter syndrome." Theresa Abalos. Accessed on August 28, 2021. https://www.theresaabalos. com/post/twelve-classical-musicians-on-imposter-syndrome

Alexander, Brenda. 2019. "American Idol Winner, Fantasia, Reflects on Her Past Suicide Attempt." Accessed August 12, 2021. Showbiz Cheatsheet. https://www.cheatsheet.com/entertainment/american-idol-winner-fantasia-reflects-on-her-past-suicide-attempt.html/

American Addiction Centers Editorial Staff. 2021. "30 Famous Musicians who have Battles Drug Addiction and Alcoholism." American Addiction Centers. Accessed August 4, 2021. https://drugabuse.com/blog/30-famous-musicians-who-have-battled-drug-addiction-and-alcoholism/

American Psychiatric Association. 2020. "What is a Substance Use Disorder?" American Psychiatric Association. Accessed August 4, 2021. https://www.psychiatry.org/patients-families/addiction/what-is-addiction

Backline. 2021. "About." Backline. Accessed September 24, 2021. https://backline.care/about/

Barnby, Joe. 2019. "A Psychologist's Take on Mental Health for Musicians." Spotify. Accessed July 23, 2021. https://artists.spotify.com/blog/a-psychologists-take-on-mental-health-for-musicians

Berkman, Seth. 2021. "50 Women who Broke Barriers in the Music Industry." Stacker. Accessed August 13, 2021. https://stacker.com/stories/6509/50-women-who-broke-barriers-music-industry

Carlson, Emily. Pasi Saari. Birgitta Burger. Petri Toiviainen. 2017. "Personality and Musical Preference Using Social-Tagging in Excerpt-Selection." Psychomusicology: Music, Mind, and Brain, 27 (3): 203-212. doi:10.1037/pmu0000183

Carson, Shelley. 2014. "Leveraging the 'mad genius' debate: why we need a neuroscience of creativity and psychopathology." NCBI. Accessed July 25, 2021. https://www.ncbi.nlm.nih.gov/pmc/articles/PMC4179620/.

Chan, Anna. 2021. "Musicians Who Have Opened Up About Their Mental Health Struggles." Accessed on July 22, 2021. Billboard. https://www.billboard.com/articles/news/9367924/musicians-mental-health-struggles/

Clance, Pauline, & Suzanne Imes. 1978. "The Impostor Phenomenon Among High Achieving Women: Dynamics and Therapeutic Intervention." Psychotherapy Theory, Research and Practice, 15(3): 241–47.

Cooksey, Kathy. 2012. "I!mposter: Understanding, Discussing, and Overcoming Imposter Syndrome." Spectrum. Cambrudge, MA. http://csma.aas.org/index.html.

Drinkaware. 2021. "Alcohol and mental health." Accessed July 25, 2021. Drinkaware. https://www.drinkaware.co.uk/facts/health-effects-of-alcohol/mental-health/alcohol-and-mental-health

Ewens, Hannah. 2016. "The Dark and Lonely World of Performance Anxiety." Vice. Accessed August 29, 2021. https://www.vice.com/en/article/rpy5qm/performance-anxiety-lonely-the-brave

Fehm, Lydia, & Katja Schmidt. 2004. "Performance anxiety in gifted adolescent musicians." Journal of Anxiety Disorders, 20, (2006): 98–109. Clinical Psychology and Psychotherapy, Technical University of Dresden, Chemnitzer Str. 46, D-01187 Dresden, Germany.

Feibel, Adam. 2020. "A Radical Act: Canadian Musicians in Conversation About Being Sober in an Industry Built on Booze." Exclaim. Accessed August 1, 2021. https://exclaim.ca/music/article/a_radical_act_canadian_musicians_in_conversation_about_being_sober_in_an_industry_built_on_booze

Female First. 2019. "Awkwafina struggled with self confidence." Female First. Accessed August 28, 2021. https://www.femalefirst.co.uk/celebrity/awkwafina-struggled-self-confidence-1203076.html?f=rss

Frehsee, Nicole. 2020. "'We Can't Have All Our Artists Die': How the Music Industry Is Fighting the Mental-Health Crisis." Rolling Stone. Accessed July 22, 2021. https://www.rollingstone.com/music/music-features/we-cant-have-all-our-artists-die-how-the-music-industry-is-fighting-the-mental-health-crisis-939171/

Friedman, Michael. 2021. "Why Musicians Make Powerful Mental Health Advocates." Psychology Today. Accessed September 24, 2021. https://www.psychologytoday.com/ca/blog/brick-brick/202106/why-musicians-make-powerful-mental-health-advocates

Gordon, Holly. 2020. "'Women are still missing in the music industry,' updated 2020 study reveals." CBC. Accessed August 13, 2021. https://www.cbc.ca/music/women-are-still-missing-in-the-music-industry-updated-2020-study-reveals-1.5436415

Gross, Sally-Anne, & George Musgrave. 2020. "Musicians are three times more likely to experience anxiety or depression than the general public, research finds." University of Westminster. Accessed July 20, 2021. https://www.westminster.ac.uk/news/musicians-are-three-times-more-likely-to-experience-anxiety-or-depression-than-the-general-public

Henriksen, Danah, Punya Mishra, & the Deep-Play Research Group. "A Pragmatic but Hopeful Conception of Creativity: a Conversation with Dr. Barbara Kerr." AECT: Column: Rethinking Technology & Creativity in the 21st Century. Arizona. January 23, 2020. https://doi.org/10.1007/s11528-020-00476-6

Hanson, David J. 2021. "Alcoholic Musicians (They Died from It, Quit, or Continue Drinking)." Alcohol Problems and Solutions. Accessed July 25, 2021. https://www.alcoholproblemsandsolutions.org/alcoholic-musicians-they-died-from-it-quit-or-continue-drinking/

Heath, Chris. 2019. "Creating While Clean." GQ. Accessed July 25, 2021. https://www.gq.com/story/clean-musicians.

Hiatt, Brian. 2017. "Paris Jackson: Life After Neverland." Rolling Stone.

Accessed August 12, 2021. https://www.rollingstone.com/music/music-features/paris-jackson-life-after-neverland-128510/

High Focus Centers. 2018. "The Dangers of Untreated Mental Illness." High Focus Centers. Accessed July 20, 2021. https://highfocuscenters.pyramidhealthcarepa.com/dangers-untreated-mental-illness/.

Hilliard, Jena. 2021. "Alcohol in Music." Alcohol Rehab Guide. Accessed July 25, 2021. https://www.alcoholrehabguide.org/alcohol/alcohol-in-popular-culture/alcohol-in-music/.

Ingraham, Christopher. 2017. "One in eight American adults is an alcoholic, study says." Washington Post. Accessed July 28, 2021. https://www.washingtonpost.com/news/wonk/wp/2017/08/11/study-one-in-eight-american-adults-are-alcoholics/

Issa-Salwe, Hamda. 2020. "Imposter Syndrome in the Music Industry if Rife, but it's not Impossible to Overcome." Mix Mag. Accessed August 13, 2021. https://mixmag.net/feature/imposter-syndrome-music-industry-mental-health

Jackman, Donnell. 2020. "Female Representation in the Music Industry Matters Too." SOS Music Media. Accessed August 13, 2021. https://sosmusicmedia.com/music-that-matters/female-representation-in-the-music-industry-matters-too

Jenning, Kell. 2017. "10 Musicians Still Alive After Insane Drug Use." List Verse. Accessed August 4, 2021. https://listverse.com/2017/07/10/10-musicians-still-alive-after-insane-drug-use/

Just, Johannes M., et al. 2016. "Drug-related celebrity deaths: A cross-sectional study." Substance Abuse Treatment, Prevention, and Policy. https://doi.org/10.1186/s13011-016-0084-z

Kaufman, James C., & Robert J. Sternberg. 2010. The Cambridge Handbook of Creativity: Creativity and Mental Illness. New York: Cambridge University Press.

Kelley, Caitlin. 2019. "The Music Industry Still Has A Long Way To Go For Gender Equality." Forbes. Accessed August 14, 2021. https://www.forbes.com/sites/caitlinkelley/2019/02/06/music-industry-study-annenberg-gender-equality/?sh=2f5b0fce5f81.

Kenny, Dianna T., & Anthony Asher. 2016. "Life Expectancy and Cause of Death in Popular Musicians: Is the Popular Musician Lifestyle the Road to Ruin?" Medical Problems of Performing Arts, (March): 37-44. http://dx.doi.org/10.21091/mppa.2016.1007

Kenny, Dianna T., & Margaret S. Osborne. 2006. "Music performance anxiety: New insights from young musicians." Advances in Cognitive Psychology, 2(2-3), 103-112.

Kheraj, Alim. 2018. "My Mental Health: 17 popstars talk about their struggles with mental illness." Accessed July 22, 2021. https://www.digitalspy.com/music/a810549/17-popstars-talk-about-their-struggles-with-mental-illness/.

Krovatin, Chris. 2020. "Remembering Jill Janus of Huntress." Kerrang. Accessed August 12, 2021. https://www.kerrang.com/features/remembering-huntress-jill-janus/

Kwon, Jake & Dakin Andone. 2019. "Goo Hara, K-pop star of Kara fame, found dead." CNN. Accessed August 12, 2021. https://www.cnn.com/2019/11/24/asia/goo-hara-kara-dead-trnd/index.html

Lau, Melody. 2019. "Why do Women Make up only 1/3 go Juno Nominees?" CBC. Accessed August 13, 2021. https://www.cbc.ca/music/junos/features/why-do-women-make-up-only-1-3-of-juno-nominees-1.4995742

Levitin, Daniel J. 2006. This is Your Brain on Music: The Science of a Human Obsession. Penguin Group. USA.

Margolis, Daniel. 2013. "25 Notable Extremes Musicians Were Driven To By Drugs." Complex. Accessed August 4, 2021. https://www.complex.com/music/2013/02/25-notable-extremes-musicians-were-driven-to-by-drugs/

Massey, Howard. 2000. Behind the Glass: Top Record Producers Tell How They Craft the Hits. Miller Freeman Books, San Francisco, pp. 295-304.

McIntosh, Steven. 2016. "Fame, fortune, fear: Why do pop stars struggle with anxiety?" BBC. Accessed August 29, 2021. https://www.bbc.com/news/entertainment-arts-37294911

New Start Recovery. 2018. "10 Famous Musicians Who Died from Substance Abuse." New Start Recovery. Accessed August 4, 2021. https://www.newstartrecovery.com/2018/01/famous-musicians-died-substance-abuse/

NIDA. 2018. "Understanding Drug Use and Addiction DrugFacts." Drug Abuse. Accessed August 4, 2021. https://www.drugabuse.gov/publications/drugfacts/understanding-drug-use-addiction

Pavitra, K.S. et al. "Creative and mental health: A profile of writers and musicians" Indian Journal of Psychiatry: Official Publication of the Indian Psychiatric Society. 2007 Jan-Mar; 49(1): 34-43. PMC2899997.

Peters, Martin. 2017. "Do Musicians Become Addicts More Often than Others?" Lanna Rehab. Accessed August 4, 2021. https://lannarehab.com/blog/do-musicians-become-addicts-more-often-than-others/

Phelps, Roger P. 2014. "Development of Musical Preference: A Comparison of Perceived Influences." Florida State University, College of Music. Published by ProQuest LLC (2014). UMI Number: 1559567.

Raine, Michael. 2019. "Music Is Facing a Mental Health Crisis." Canadian Musician. Accessed September 24, 2021. https://www.canadianmusician.com/post/music-is-facing-a-mental-health-crisis

Roberts, Nikki. 2021. "Girl Power: Fighting Gender Discrimination in the Music Industry." Fourteen East Mag. Accessed September 3, 2021. http://fourteeneastmag.com/index.php/2018/07/13/girl-power-fighting-gender-discrimination-in-the-music-industry/

Roberts, S.E., B. Jaremin, and K. Lloyd. 2012. "High-risk Occupations for Suicide." Psychological Medicine 43, 1231-1240. doi:10.1017/S0033291712002024

Saunders, Gemma. 2020. "Is it Harder for Females to Make it into the Pop Industry?" Open Mic. Accessed August 11, 2021. https://www.openmicuk.co.uk/advice/is-it-harder-for-females-to-make-it-into-the-pop-industry/

Silence the Shame. 2021. "Who We Are." Silence the Shame. Accessed September 24 2021. https://silencetheshame.com/who-we-are/mission. html

Simon, Samantha. 2017. "25 Stars Who Suffer from Imposter Syndrome." In Style. Accessed August 28, 2021. https://www.instyle.com/celebrity/stars-imposter-syndrome?

Skanse, Richard. 1998. "Plasmatics' Wendy O. Williams Commits Suicide." Rolling Stone. Accessed August 12, 2021. https://www.rollingstone.com/music/music-news/plasmatics-wendy-o-williams-commits-suicide-187613/

Small, C. (1997). Musicking: a ritual in social space. On the sociology of music education, 1-12.

Tan, Yvette & Wonsang Kim. 2019. "Sulli: The woman who rebelled against the K-pop world." BBC. Accessed Aug 12, 2021. https://www.bbc.com/news/world-asia-50051575

The Associated Press. 2020. "Grammys CEO says She was Ousted After ReportingHarassment." CBC. Accessed August 13, 2021. https://www.cbc.ca/news/entertainment/ousted-grammys-ceo-1.5435624

The Band. 1970. "Stage Fright." From the Album Stage Fright. Capitol Records, United States, SW-425.

The Task Force. 2019. "Final Report of the Recording Academy Task Force on Diversity and Inclusion." https://www.grammy.com/sites/com/files/final_task_force_report.pdf

Wassenberg, Anya. 2019. "It's Time To Talk About Classical Music's Mental Health Problem." Accessed July 23, 2021. https://www.ludwig-van.com/toronto/2019/02/25/feature-its-time-to-talk-about-classical-musics-mental-health-problem/

Weinberger, Norman, M. 2006. "Music and the Brain: What is the secret of music's strange power? Seeking an answer, scientists are piecing together a picture of what happens in the brains of listeners and musicians." Scientific American. Accessed September 17, 2021. https://www.scientificamerican.com/article/music-and-the-brain-2006-09/

White, Scott. 2018. "The Link Between Drugs and Music Explained by Science." The Conversation. Accessed August 4, 2021. https://theconversation.com/the-link-between-drugs-and-music-explained-by-science-89132

Wong, Jessica. 2019. "Changing the tune on tortured artists and musicians' mental health." CBC. Accessed September 24 2021. https://www.cbc.ca/news/entertainment/musicians-mental-health-1.5322852

World Health Organization. 2021. "Suicide." Accessed August 11, 2021. https://www.who.int/news-room/fact-sheets/detail/suicide

Vincent, Peter. 2014. "Why musicians battle alcoholism behind closed doors." Accessed August 1, 2021. https://www.stuff.co.nz/entertainment/music/9629131/Why-musicians-battle-alcoholism-behind-closed-doors

Zoladz, Lindsay. 2021. "She's Marianne Faithfull, Damn It. And She's (Thankfully) Still Here." NY Times. Accessed August 6, 2021. https://www.nytimes.com/2021/04/22/arts/music/marianne-faithfull-she-walks-in-beauty.html

www.ingramcontent.com/pod-product-compliance
Lightning Source LLC
Chambersburg PA
CBHW030853270326
41928CB00008B/1359